S K E T C H I N G

WITH

MARKERS

SECOND EDITION

SKETCHING

WITH

MARKERS

SECOND EDITION

THOMAS C. WANG

VNR VAN NOSTRAND REINHOLD
New York

Copyright © 1993 by Van Nostrand Reinhold
First published by Prentice Hall Press in 1986.
Library of Congress Catalog Card Number 92-4326
ISBN 0-442-00491-5

I(T)P   Van Nostrand Reinhold is an International Thomson Publishing company.
         ITP logo is a trademark under license.

Printed in the United States of America

Van Nostrand Reinhold   ITP Germany
115 Fifth Avenue   Königswinterer Str. 418
New York, NY 10003   53227 Bonn
                                    Germany

International Thomson Publishing   International Thomson Publishing Asia
Berkshire House,168-173   38 Kim Tian Rd., #0105
High Holborn, London WC1V 7AA   Kim Tian Plaza
England   Singapore 0316

Thomas Nelson Australia   International Thomson Publishing Japan
102 Dodds Street   Kyowa Building, 3F
South Melbourne 3205   2-2-1 Hirakawacho
Victoria, Australia   Chiyada-Ku, Tokyo 102
                                    Japan

Nelson Canada
1120 Birchmount Road
Scarborough, Ontario
M1K 5G4, Canada

16 15 14 13 12 11 10 9 8 7 6 5 4 3 2

Library of Congress Cataloging in Publication Data
Wang, Thomas C.
    Sketching with markers / Thomas C. Wang.—2nd ed.
        p.   cm.
    Originally published : New York : Prentice Hall, © 1986.
    Includes index.
    ISBN 0-442-00491-5
    1. Dry marker drawing—Technique. I. Originally published : New York : Prentice Hall, © 1986.
    Title.
NC878.W36   1992
741.2'6—dc20   92-4326
                         CIP

*To Joseph, Andrew,
and, Matthew*

Title: New Territories, Hong Kong
Original size: 9 x 17 inches
Medium: Pilot razor point and watercolors
Technique: wash

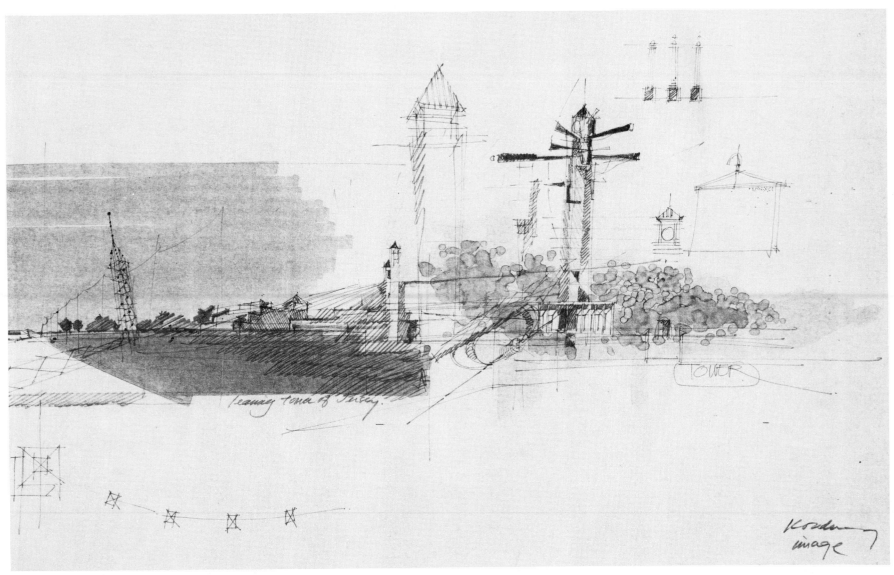

Title: Design Study
Original size: 14 x 36 inches
Medium: markers on yellow tracing paper
Technique: line drawing with markers
highlight, some mixing

CONTENTS

PREFACE

Markers are probably one of the most popular sketching media. They are versatile, expressive, colorful, and, above all, easy to use. Yet, because of their ability to adapt to a wide range of drawing techniques, markers are still used primarily as a substitute for other traditional sketching media. For example, the fine-point marker can be used to duplicate the performance of an ink pen. Likewise, the rainbow selection of Flair pens is used like an ordinary color-pencil set. Markers are popular because of their ease in handling and simplicity, rather than for their uniqueness, construction, and range of nib sizes and inks. This, unfortunately, does not encourage the development of drawing techniques specifically for markers. If this pattern persists, markers may always hold a second-fiddle position to pen and pencil, which have an ancient and respectable heritage.

This book emphasizes the unusual versatility of this remarkable drawing instrument and demonstrates its unique ability to combine its own quality harmoniously with many other media such as water-color, pen, pencil, and ink. It is my intent to encourage the use and increase the awareness of the marker as a superior sketching tool with unique qualities that can only be expressed thoroughly through the art of sketching.

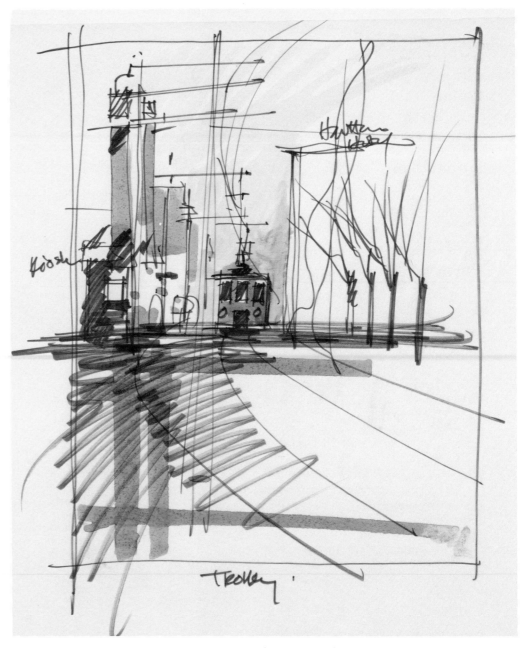

Title: Urban Spatial Study
Original size: 8 x 11 inches
Medium: markers on white tracing paper
Technique: quick sketch

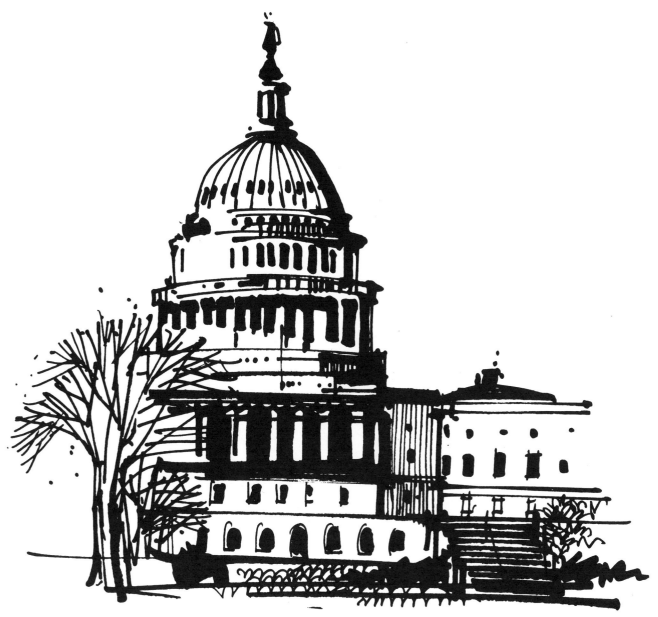

INTRODUCTION

A Sketch

A sketch, by definition, is a rough drawing that represents the chief features of an object or scene. To be more precise, a sketch should accomplish the following:

- capture the essence of an image
- give a simplified version of a complex scene
- provide an abstract graphic description of reality
- create a graphic expression with the minimum amount of lines, tones, and textures
- serve as a quick reproduction process

Title: Washington, D.C.
Original size: 9 x 13 inches
Medium: black Eberhard Faber (pointed-nib) on Aquabee felt-tip-marker paper
Technique: quick, semibroad strokes

Degree of Abstraction

A sketch is a form of graphic shorthand. The primary objective is to record the image quickly with a variety of lines and tones. Despite its simple, semiabstract appearance, the theme (subject matter) of a sketch must be recognizable. The relative proportion and scale of all major components must be accurately portrayed.

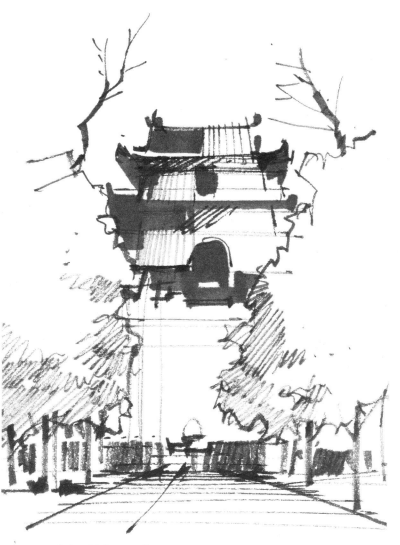

a   abstract interpretation

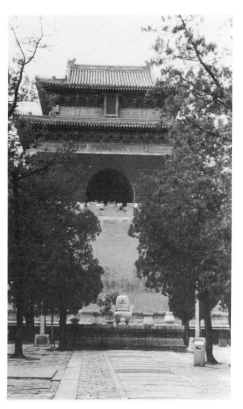

b   reality

1

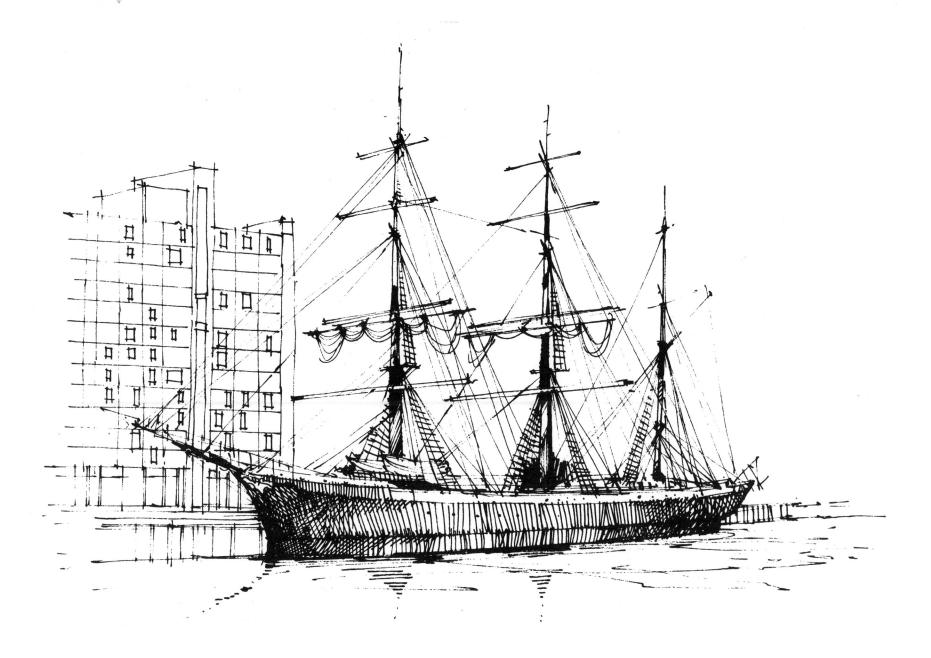

Title: Boats
Original size: 9 x 13 inches
Medium: Pilot razor point on bristol board
Technique: combination of line and
line texture

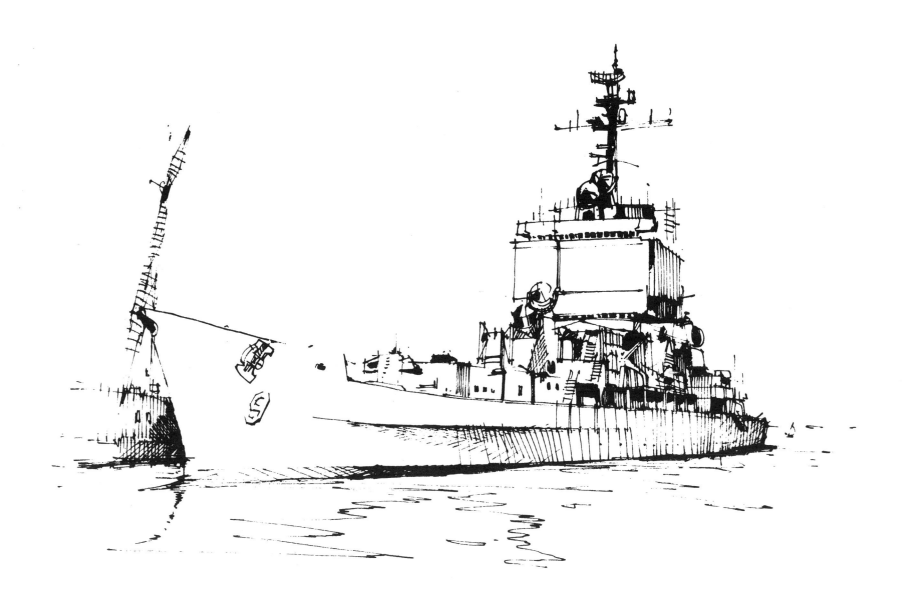

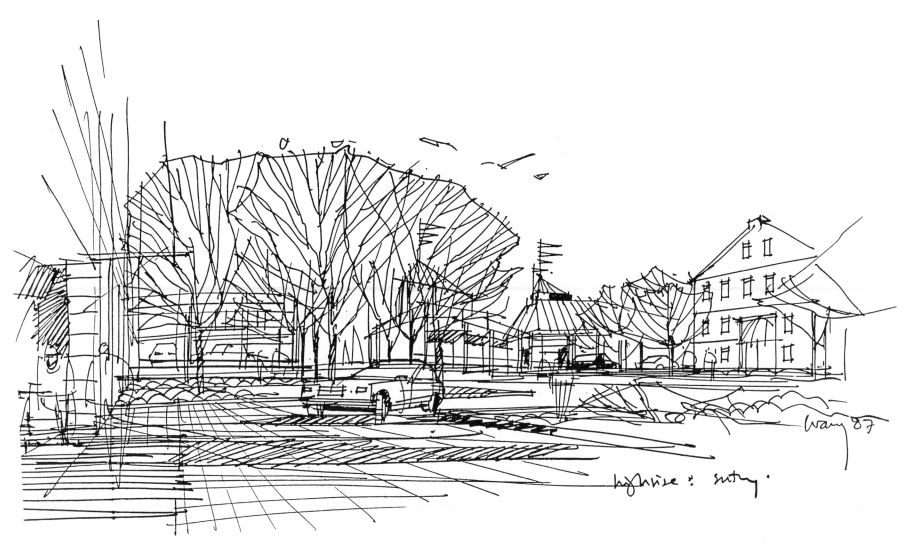

Title: Design Study
Original size: 11 x 17
Medium: thin felt-tip markers on
white tracing paper
Technique: line drawing

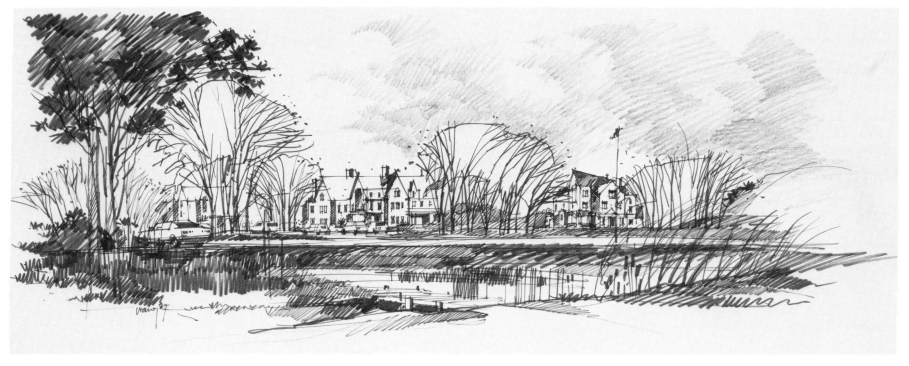

Title: Housing Study
Original size: 11 x 20 inches
Medium: felt-tip markers and pencil
on white tracing paper
Technique: line and tone sketch

EQUIPMENT

The style and quality of markers are constantly improving. Henry C. Pitz, in his book *Sketching with the Felt-tip Pen* (1959), referred to the felt-tip pen as "the new tool." At that time it was a new invention and was certainly a novelty to artists. The marker has since evolved into one of the most popular drawing media, replacing pen, pencil, and other color media. It is widely used for a number of good reasons: it is simple to work with; it dries fast and it usually does not smudge; it comes in numerous pre-mixed colors and a variety of tip designs; its nib is often soft and penetrating; and, above all, the marker is convenient.

The marker also has its drawbacks. It is not an inexpensive medium. It also has a relatively short shelf life. The penetrating effect of most markers requires special paper, and bleeding is extremely difficult to predict and control. The convenience of premixed color eliminates the creative possibilities of color mixing. Over all, its ease in handling is welcomed by most students, who think of it as a lazy man's tool.

The marker should be looked upon as a unique medium. It is neither pen nor pencil and should not be used as such. It has a unique tip that responds to pressure, surface conditions, and fluid characteristics. These features make markers excellent sketching tools. Therefore an *intimate* understanding of their characteristics is vital to successful sketching.

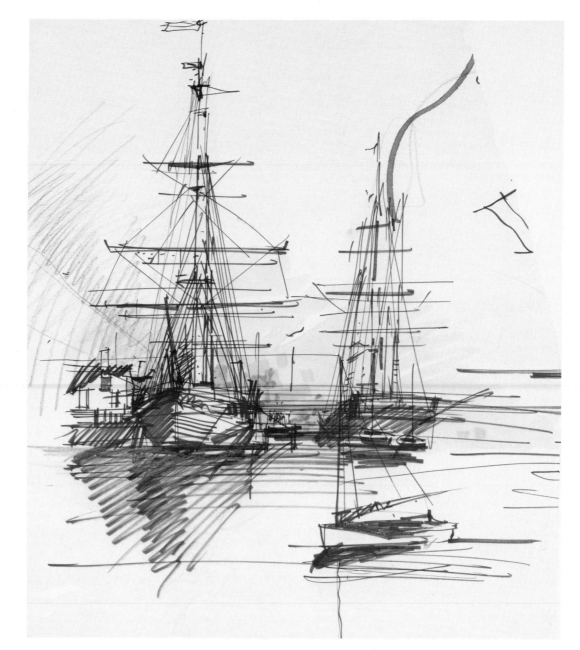

Title: Tall Ship
Original size: 11 x 17 inches
Medium: felt-tip markers on white tracing paper
Technique: line drawing, textural shading

Types of Markers

There are several common types of markers with which one should be familiar:

- Wide-nib (soft-tip) marker, which has a felt tip approximately ¼ inch long and ⅛ inch wide. It is responsive to pressure and twisting and it produces smooth and consistent broad strokes.
- Pointed-nib (bullet-point) marker, which has a semisoft, conical felt tip. It responds to pressure and to various positions and is capable of producing a variety of line widths. It works like a soft pencil.
- Fine-point marker, which has a sharp, hard tip of either felt or nylon. It is an excellent ink-pen substitute when new. The point, however, is subject to pressure and wear.
- Fine-line marker, which comes in a small pen-size container for easy holding and is ideal for drawing details. The new ballpoint or hard nylon nib produces broken lines when moved rapidly and tends to scratch the paper surface. This latter type is not ideal for general sketching purposes.

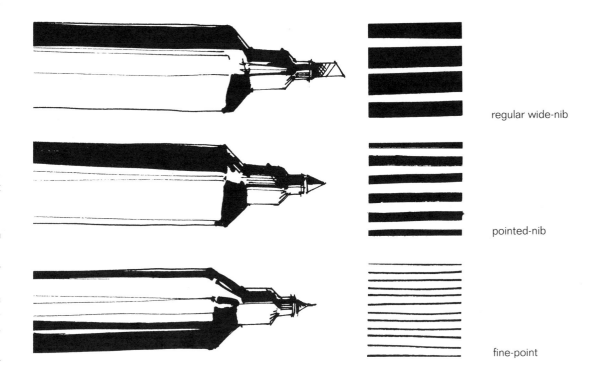

regular wide-nib

pointed-nib

fine-point

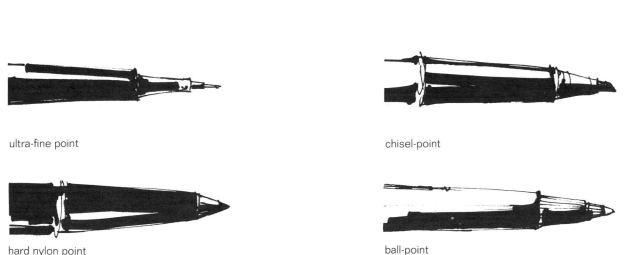

ultra-fine point

chisel-point

types of fine-line markers

hard nylon point

ball-point

7

Paper

The character of a sketch relies a great deal upon the surface on which it is drawn. Pay close attention to the type of paper you use and understand its characteristics as you get acquainted with your markers. There are many choices, and you should discover your favorites by a process of trial and error. In general, avoid papers that can be penetrated and that bleed easily, unless you desire a special effect. The beginner should try Aquabee felt-tip-marker paper, which has a waxy coating on the reverse side, or Aquabee magic visualizer. Advanced and daring sketchers can try watercolor paper, tracing paper, rice paper, or even white dinner napkins. Your creativity and imagination are your only limits, and appropriateness is a matter of taste.

Some popular varieties of paper are the following:

- Bristol board is smooth, thick-bonded, with a high gloss, and is excellent for fine-line drawing.
- Blueprint paper is soft, absorbent, and loose in fiber; bleeding and penetration are difficult to control.
- Rice paper has a coarse texture, is highly absorbent, and exhibits an unpredictable bleeding pattern. It has an explosive effect when wet. There is a vast range in quality.
- Watercolor paper, which has a coarse, rough surface, will wear out fine-nib markers. It has an excellent surface for tone and mixed media, but it is not suited for line drawing.

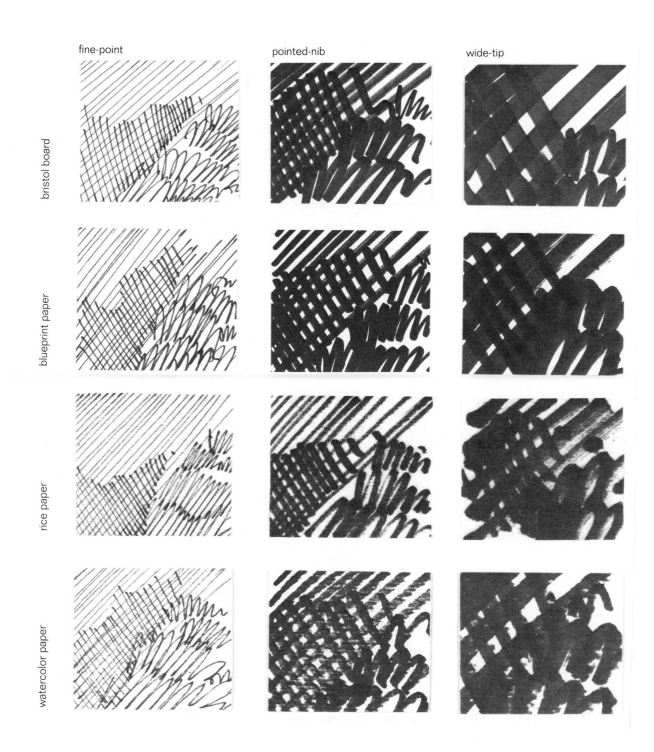

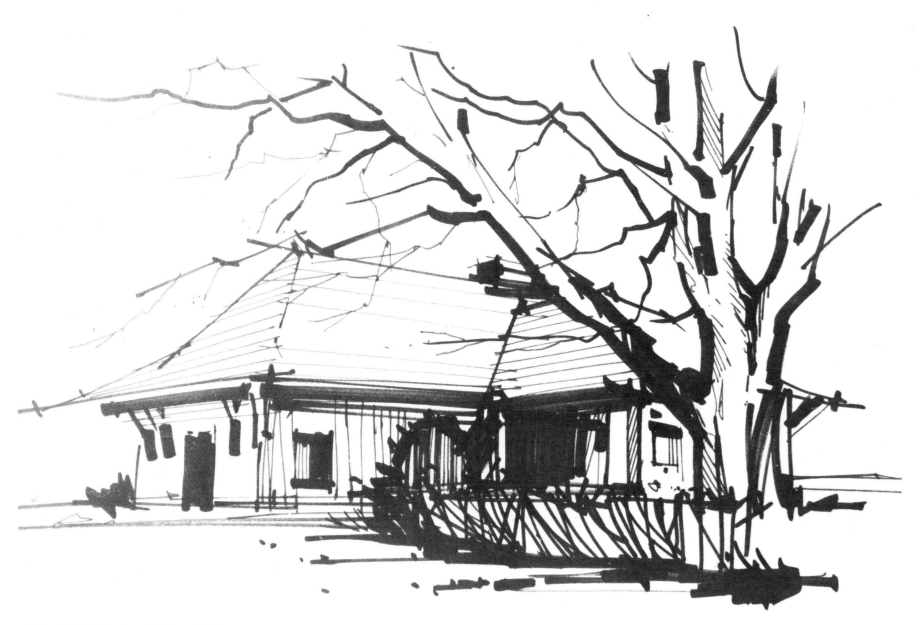

Title: H. H. Richardson's Railroad Station,
Easton, Massachusetts
Original size: 9 x 12 inches
Medium: Eberhard Faber (pointed-nib)
on bristol board
Technique: line drawing

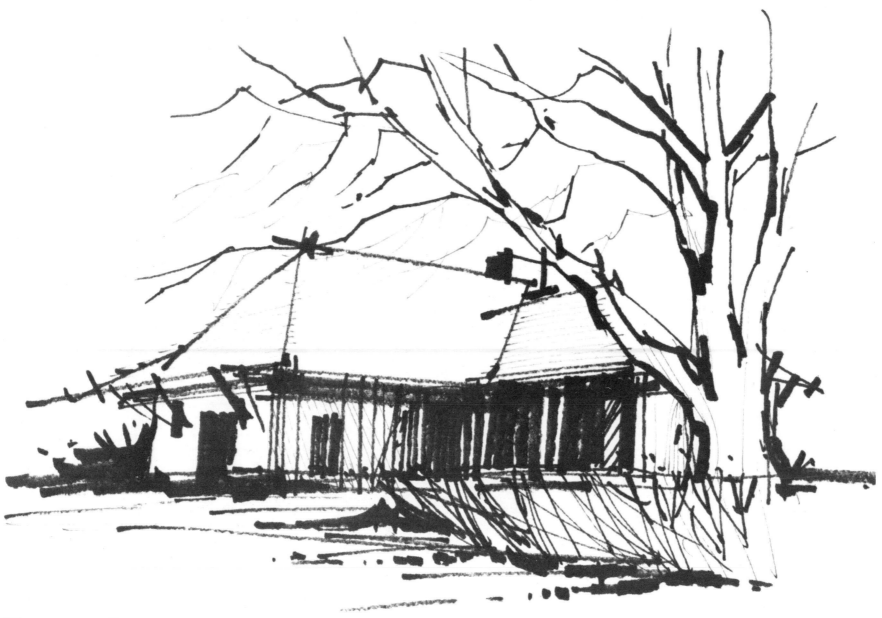

Title: same as page 19
Original size: same
Medium: Eberhard Faber (pointed-nib)
on watercolor paper
Technique: line drawing

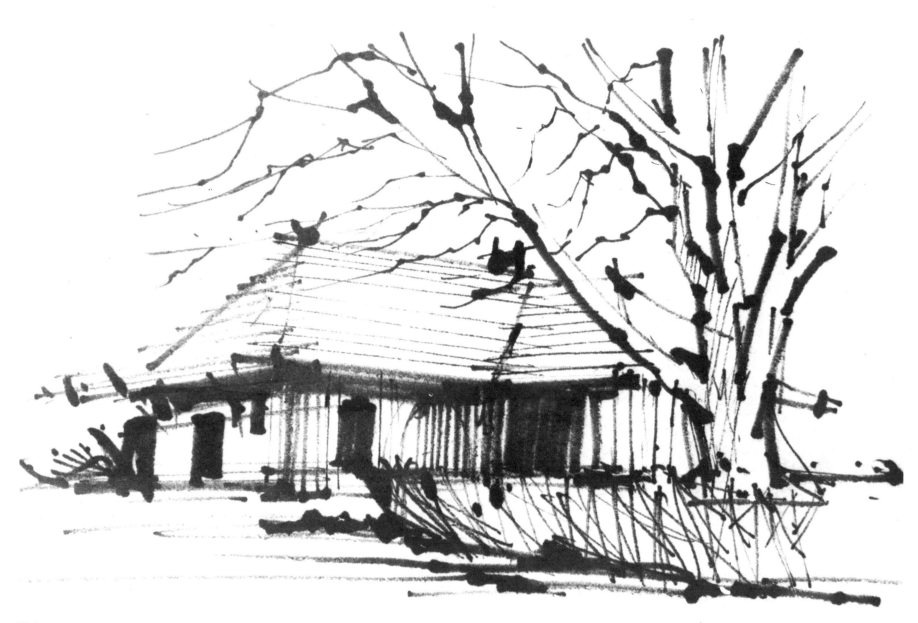

Title: same as page 19
Original size: same
Medium: Eberhard Faber (pointed-nib)
on rice paper
Technique: line drawing

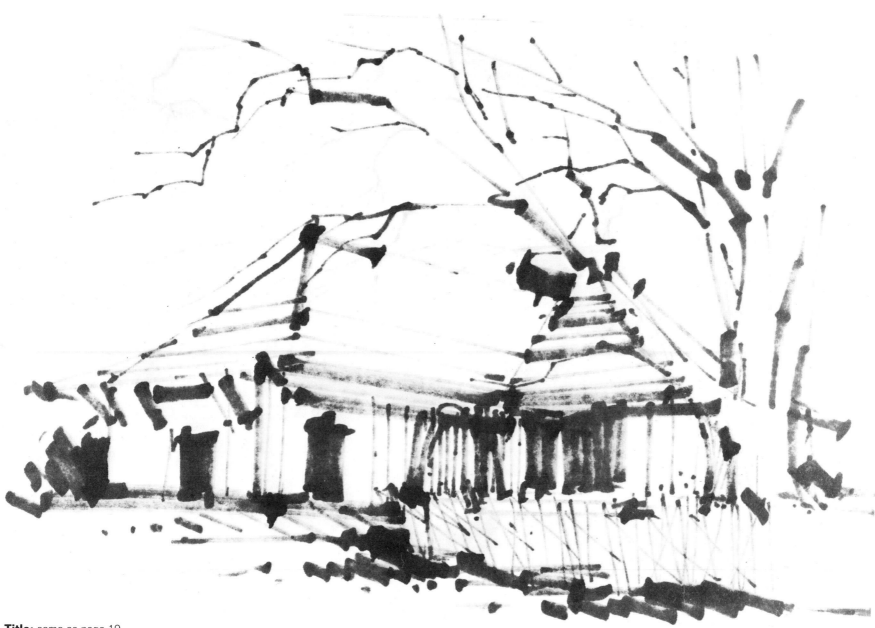

Title: same as page 19
Original size: same
Medium: Eberhard Faber (pointed-nib)
on Aquabee felt-tip-marker paper
Technique: line drawing

Safety Concerns

Due to the chemical compound of the color base in markers, most markers are toxic and harmful to the user's health. The fumes emitted during the application of certain markers can cause dizziness and other side effects. Many markers now carry warning labels informing users about the potential health hazard. In addition, many markers today are environmentally safe and child friendly. Unfortunately, these "safe" markers do not come in a large selection of colors and nib sizes. The selection is limited and the color effect less than desirable.

Before we see a complete change to all environmentally safe products, the most important work-related criteria in ensuring health and safety is to work in a well ventilated space. A small fan is also indispensable. It should be strategically placed to clear the fumes without disrupting the drawing surface. When working with benzene or other mixing fluid, a mask and a strong fan are musts. These fluids are extremely flammable and should be stored away from flame. In addition, use your common sense to make sure that your health and safety—as well as the health and safety of those around you—are not jeopardized.

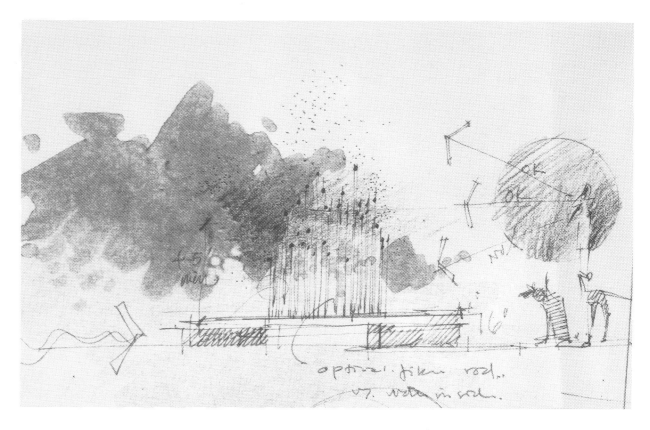

Title: Fountain Study
Original size: 6 x 8 inches
Medium: color markers on tracing paper
Technique: quick sketch

BASIC TECHNIQUE: LINE

A line is a straight or curved connection between two points. It defines a spatial edge that separates a mass from a space. It delineates detail and renders the effects of a light source. It brings out the three-dimensional quality of an object. Line can be expressed in many ways: according to width, length, density, orientation, and appearance. Marker line produces texture and tone easily due to nib variations. Line quality is an evaluation of line function, type, movement, and expression. A line drawn with a marker is inherently and characteristically different from one drawn with a pencil. A marker line is controlled by the size and condition of the nib and the type and quantity of the ink storage. The art of working with markers is also unique because of the nib construction and size variation. For example, ink flow in a new marker is quite consistent; in order to lighten the tone, you must switch to a lighter-color or a semi-dry marker. Variation of hand pressure is not applied to control tone, but rather to control line width and movement.

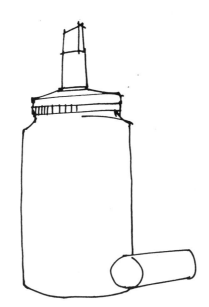

line profile

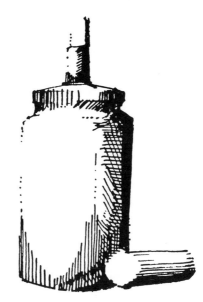

texture

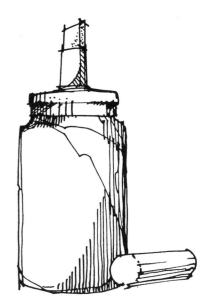

line and texture

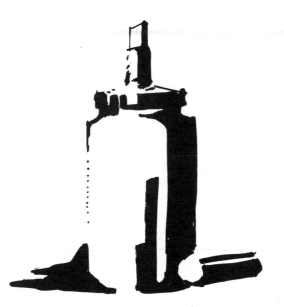

tone (high contrast)

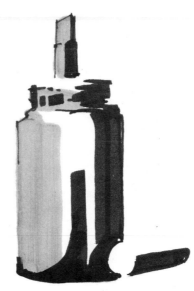

tone (with grays)

Types of Lines

There are many types of lines:

- lines drawn with even pressure, pulled from left to right (fine point) (Figure a on page 16)
- lines drawn in a series of short pauses at random intervals, with the marker remaining on the paper (fine point)
- lines drawn in a series of short pauses at random intervals, with the marker removed from the paper (fine point)
- short strokes
- lines drawn with a pointed-nib marker, varying the pressure on the point (Figure b on page 16)
- lines drawn with a pointed-nib marker, twisting and varying the pressure
- casual, short nondirectional strokes (fine point)
- casual short strokes drawn with a pointed-nib marker
- lines drawn with a semi-dry pointed-nib marker
- wide-tip-marker strokes
- series of short, casual arcs
- series of small, flat loops

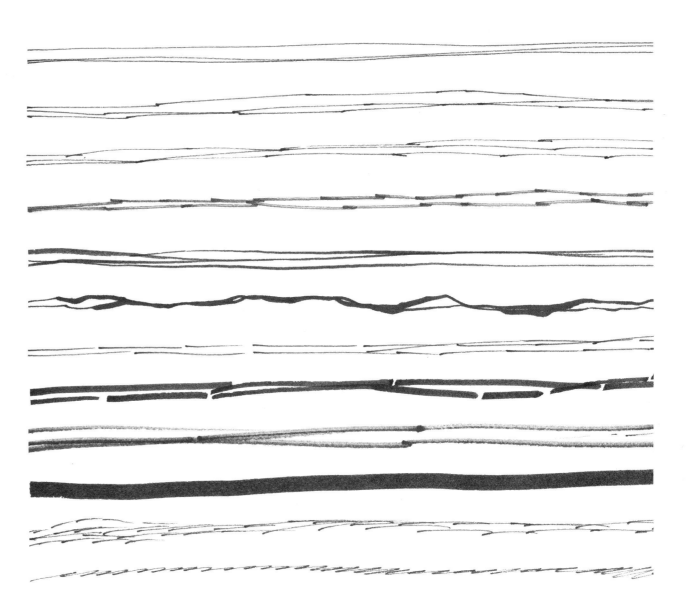

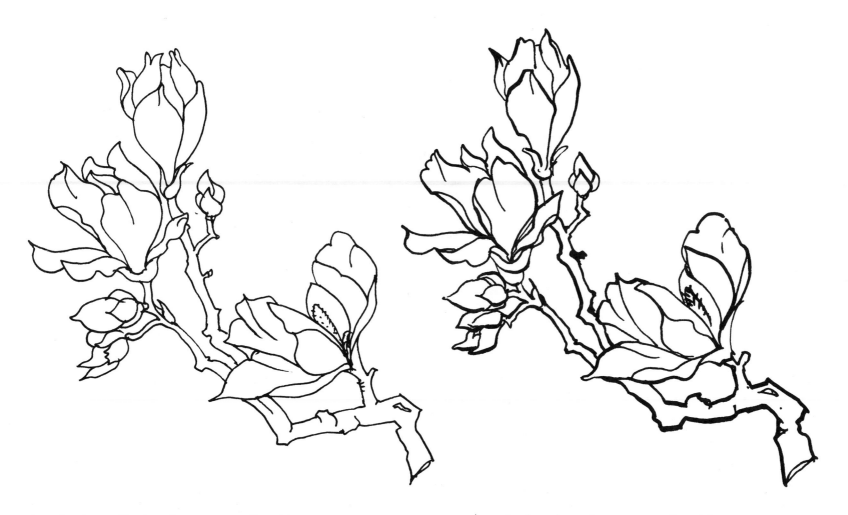

a   line drawn without varying pressure on the point

b   line drawn by varying pressure on the point

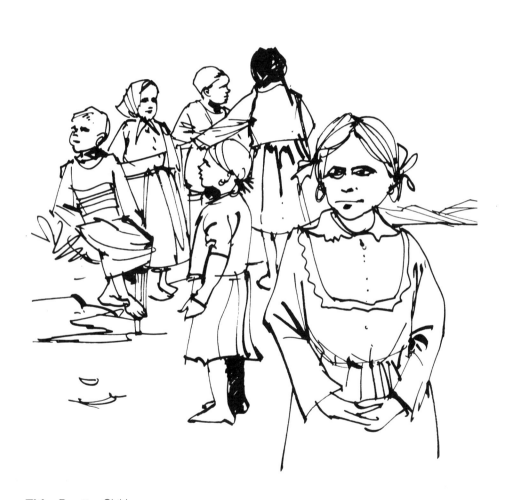
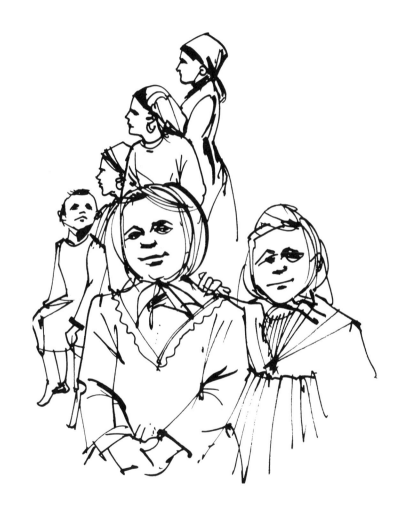

Title: Egyptian Children
Original size: 8½ x 11 inches
Medium: Eberhard Faber (pointed-nib)
on bond
Technique: line

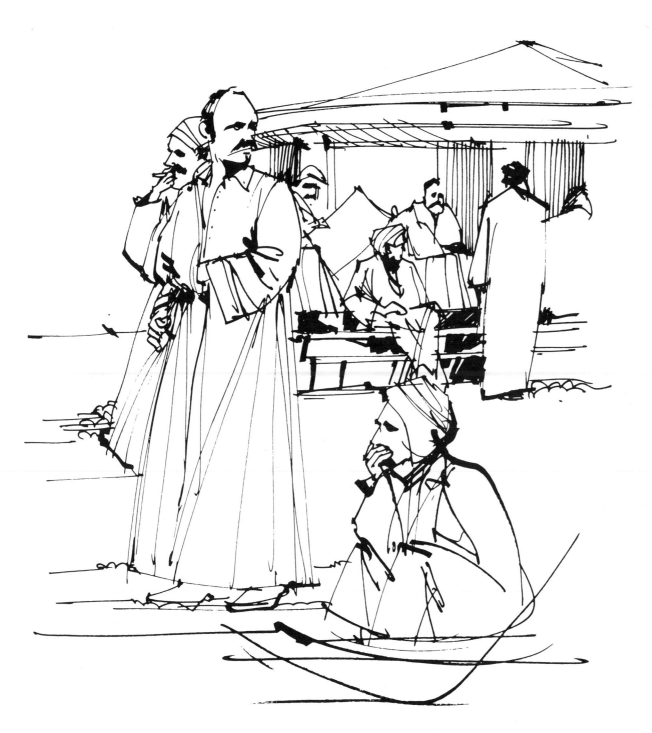

Title: Egyptian Men
Original size: 8½ x 11 inches
Medium: Eberhard Faber (pointed-nib)
on bond
Technique: line

Wide-Nib-Marker Lines

The wide-nib marker is a unique drawing tool because of its broad ½- to ¼-inch felt nib. As a tone medium, it is ideal for filling in areas between lines. As a line medium, the broad strokes can quickly define an area and therefore simplify the sketch. Semitransparent juxtapositioning of broad strokes injects new life and character into a drawing by giving it contrast and motion. The application of the wide-nib marker to sketching is similar to the use of pastels and oil-painting brushes: all have a premeasured applicator. It is this characteristic that makes markers unique. Rather than simply using them to fill in areas, a task that can be done with many other color media, this characteristic should be creatively exploited.

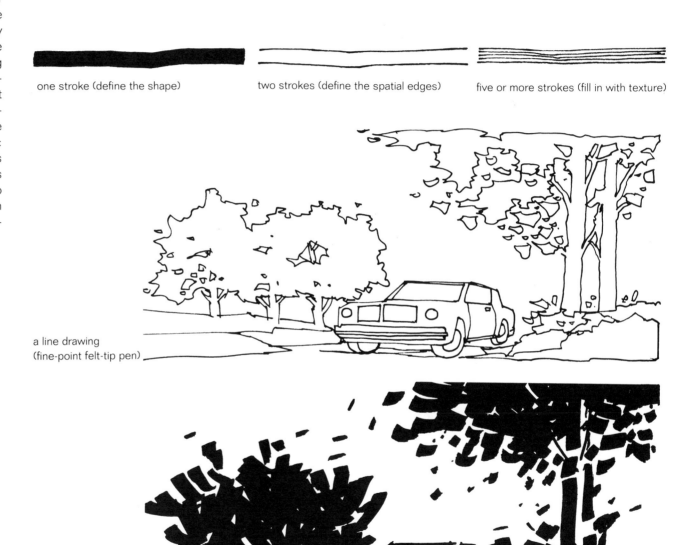

one stroke (define the shape)

two strokes (define the spatial edges)

five or more strokes (fill in with texture)

a line drawing
(fine-point felt-tip pen)

a line drawing
(wide-nib marker)

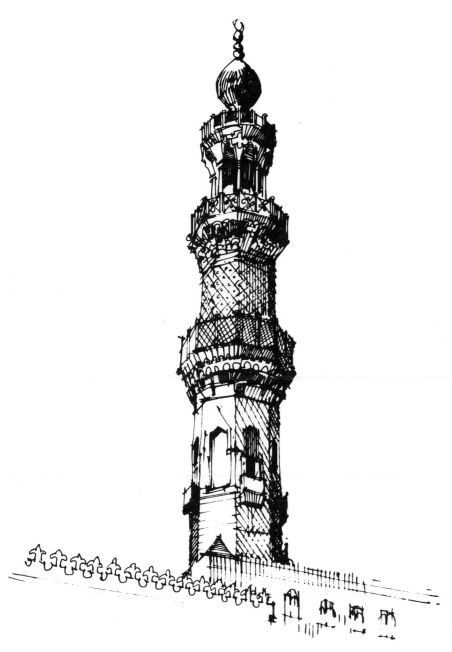

Title: Mosque in Cairo, Egypt
Original size: 9 x 12 inches
Medium: Pilot razor point on bristol board
Technique: line texture

Title: Palace at Heliopolis, Egypt
Original size: 9 x 12 inches
Medium: Pilot razor point on bristol board
Technique: line texture

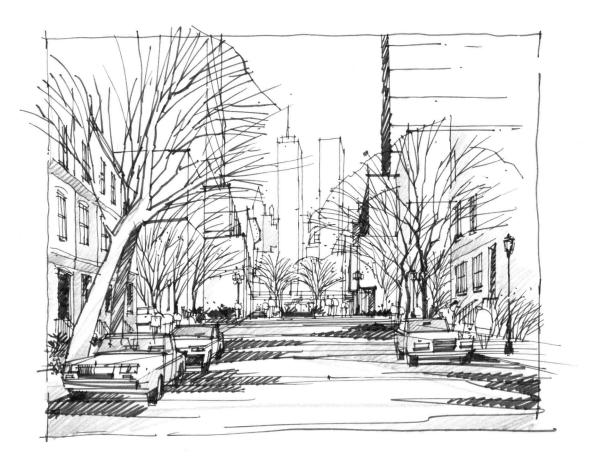

Title: Street Study
Original size: 8 x 11 inches
Medium: felt-tip markers and pencil on white tracing paper
Technique: line and tone drawing

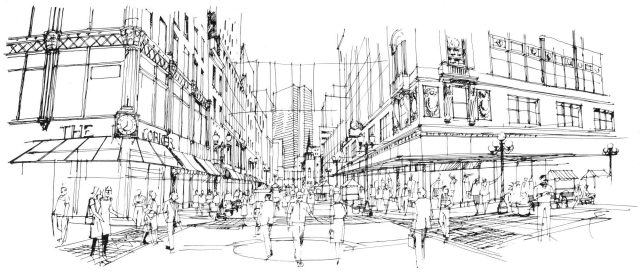

Title: Downtown
Original size: 14 x 30 inches
Medium: felt-tip markers on yellow tracing paper
Technique: line drawing

BASIC TECHNIQUE: TEXTURE

Texture consists of semiabstract graphic symbols that signify the surface or material of the drawn object. The tonal effect of texture also helps to enhance the sensation of depth in two-dimensional representation.

There are two basic types of texture: lines and dots (screens). The meaning and effect of these textures depend upon the interpretation of size, overall density, line orientation, spacing, and overall tonal effect.

Line texture can be divided into parallel and nonparallel (better known as "squiggles" or "scribbles") patterns. Parallel lines (including cross-hatching) are often used to express vertical or horizontal planes that have a smooth surface. The spacing between lines and the line width should be kept consistent throughout a rendered plane. It is an abstract expression, and the artist should not be too concerned with the literal meaning of the material. Nonparallel lines are a bundle of loose threads. The line width and the spacing are often varied in order to achieve a desired density and tonal effect. These lines are ideal symbols to depict vegetation and for undulating surfaces.

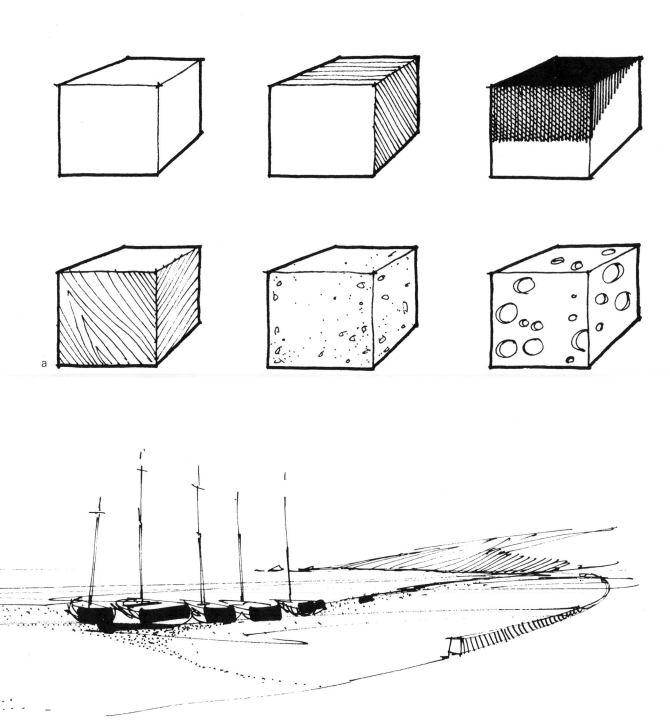

Types of Texture

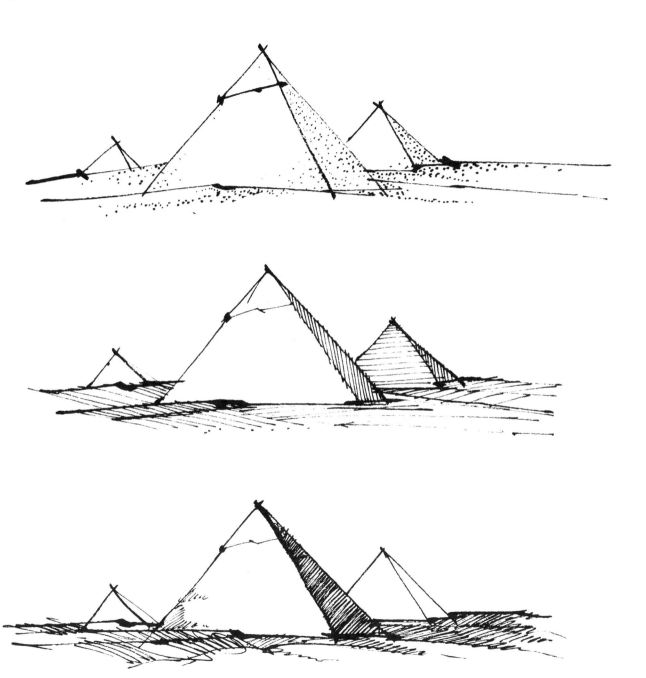

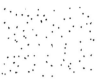

dots

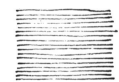

lines (parallel)

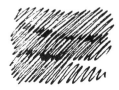

lines (scribbles)

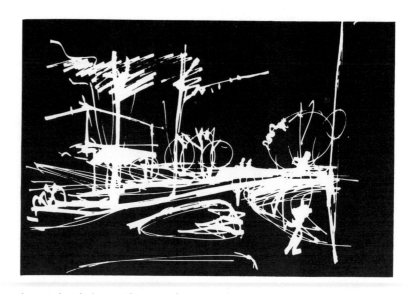

layout sketch done with a pentel

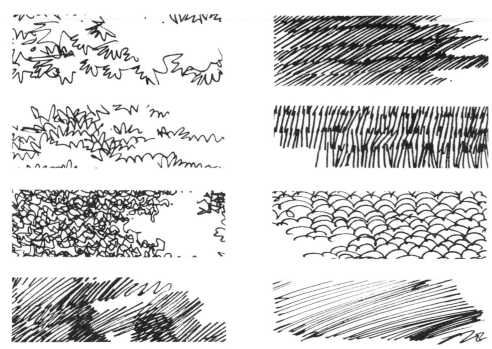

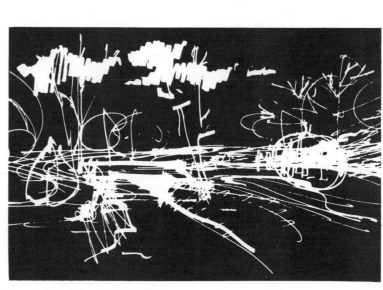

texture (scribbles) drawn with a fine-point marker

layout sketch done with a pentel

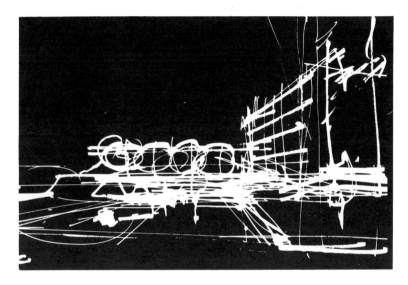

layout sketch done with a pentel

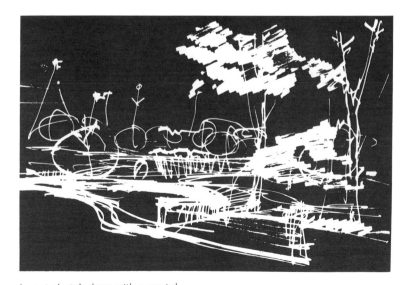

layout sketch done with a pentel

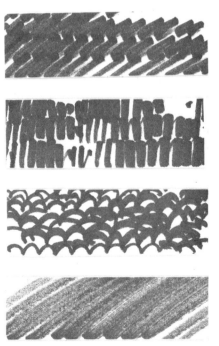
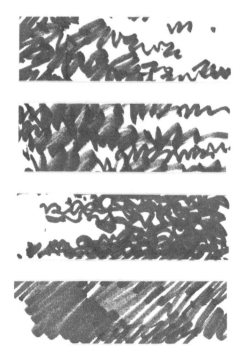

texture (scribbles) drawn with a pointed-nib marker

Parallel Line, Texture and Direction

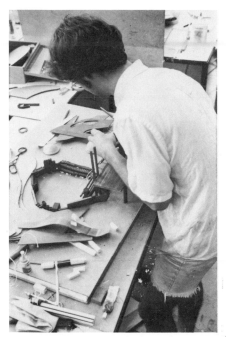

photograph

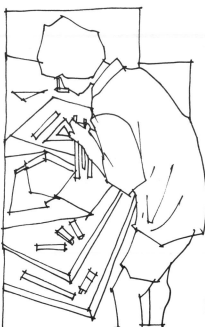

profile line

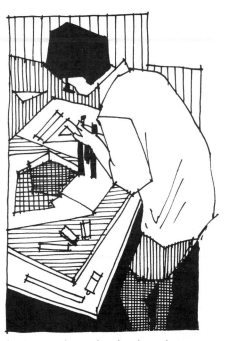

line texture (cross-hatching) used to create tone and separate depth; lines parallel with the edges of paper

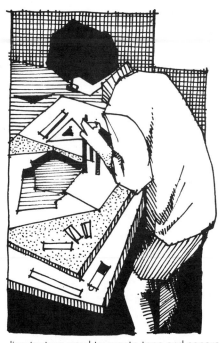

line texture used to create tone and separate depth; lines parallel with different surfaces

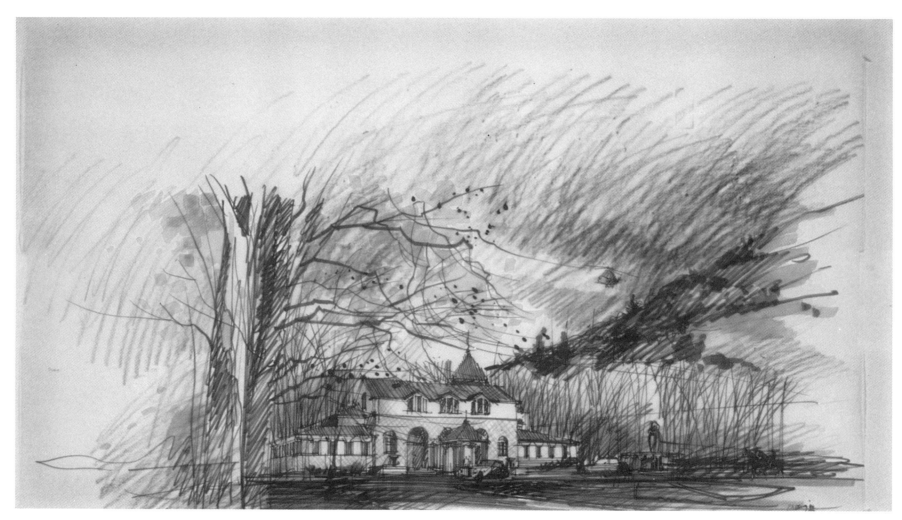

Title: Birkshire Spa Study I
Original size: 18 x 24 inches
Medium: color markers and felt-tip
markers on white tracing paper
Technique: color markers over felt-tip
line sketch

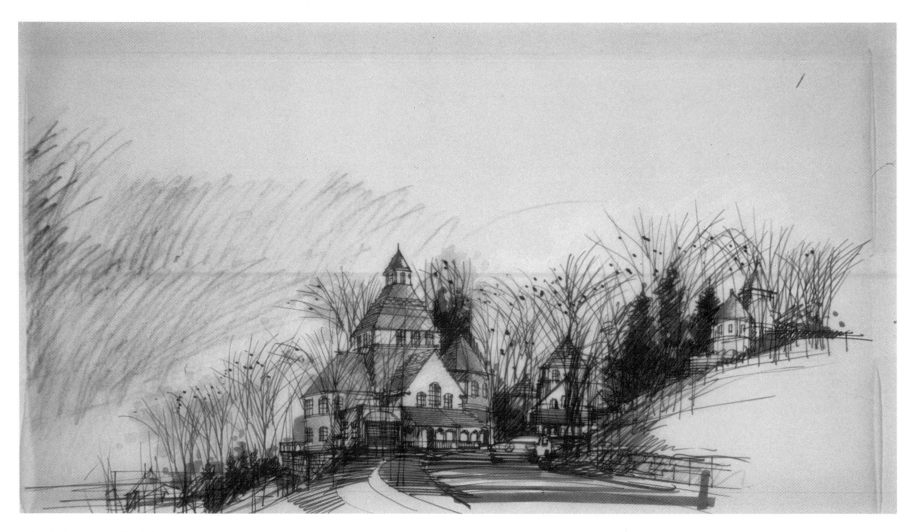

Title: Birkshire Spa Study II
Original size: 18 x 24 inches
Medium: color markers and felt-tip
markers on white tracing paper
Technique: color markers over felt-tip
line sketch

BASIC TECHNIQUE: TONE

Tonal value can be achieved either through textural density or varying line widths. It is used in most sketches to increase the feeling of depth and to bring out the three-dimensional quality of the various components. Generally speaking, the sun side should be brighter (less dense) than the shaded side. The shadow pattern is often rendered in black, dark gray, or dense, thick lines. Tonal contrast is important in reading depth, so a substantial white area should be preplanned and reserved in order to achieve this special effect.

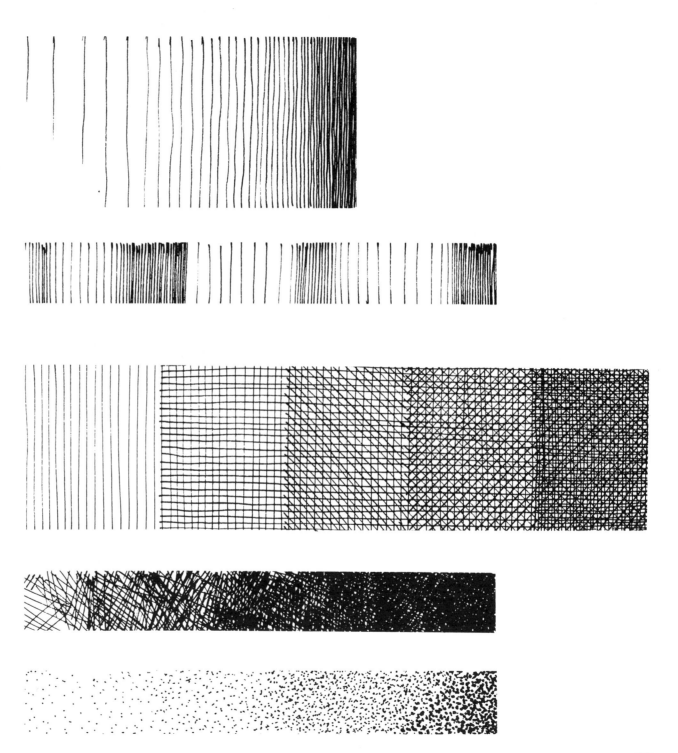

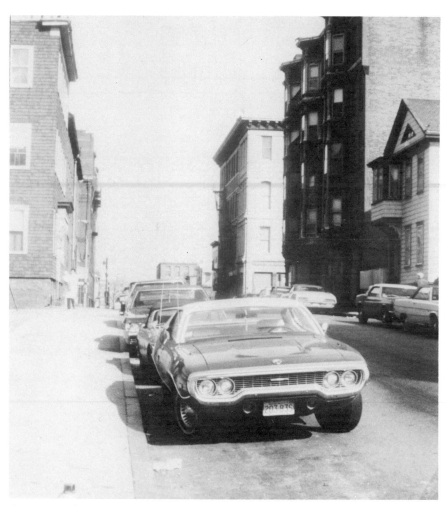

photograph of a street

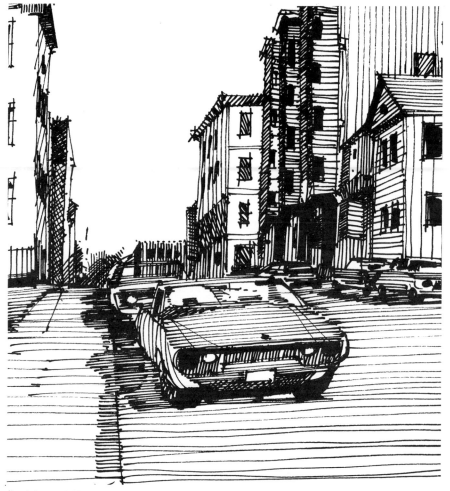

line interpretation

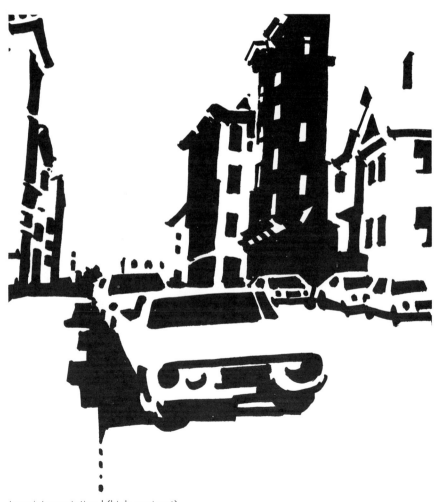

tone interpretation I (high contrast)

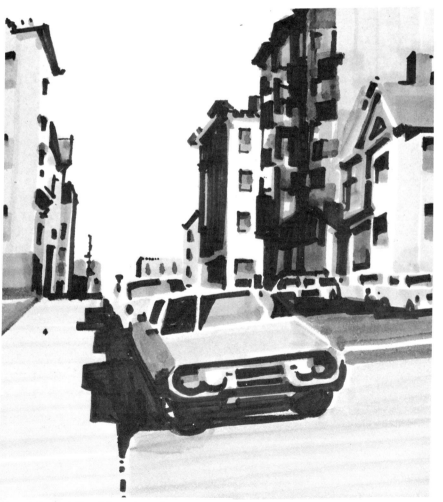

tone interpretation II (gray tones)

Gray Markers

A gray marker is ideal for the creation of tone. However, the result is often unpredictable and the effects are inconsistent. The warm-gray and cool-gray ranges are excellent tone media. There is not much perceivable difference between two consecutive grays: for better and sharper differentiation, try skipping at least one shade. Warm-gray is better for blending with other colors. Cool-gray has a metallic appearance and tends to stand out.

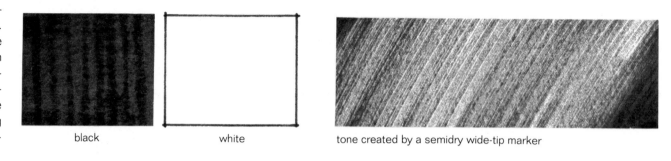

black   white   tone created by a semidry wide-tip marker

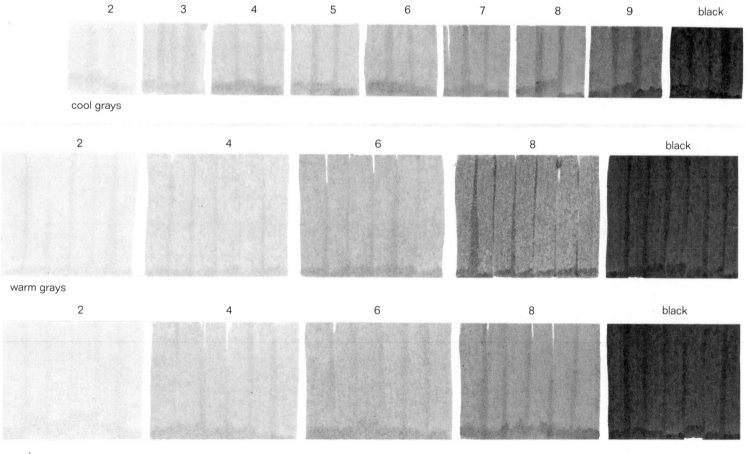

2   3   4   5   6   7   8   9   black

cool grays

2   4   6   8   black

warm grays

2   4   6   8   black

cool grays

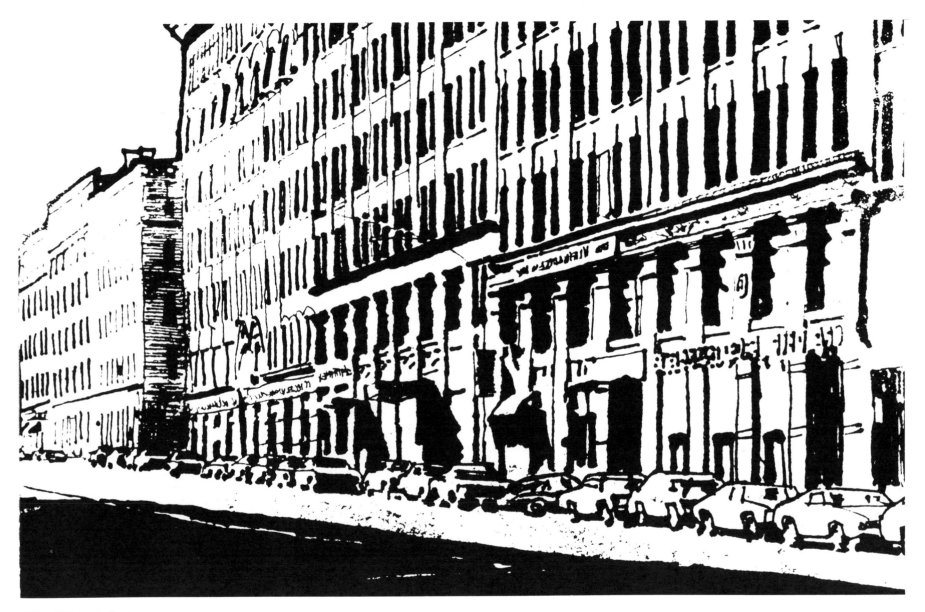

Title: Building in Boston
Original size: 24 x 30 inches
Medium: black marker on brown
butcher paper
Technique: copy from slide; black marker
used to produce the high-contrast look; use
of line to define spatial edges is minimal

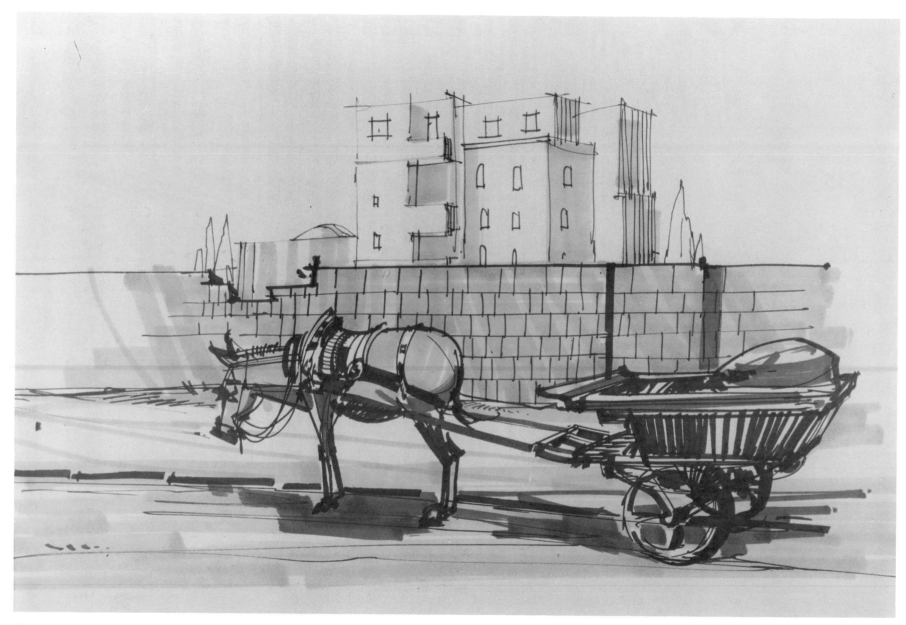

Title: Egyptian Donkey Cart
Original size: 9 x 12 inches
Medium: black and gray markers on
bristol board
Technique: line drawing and broad
marker strokes

34

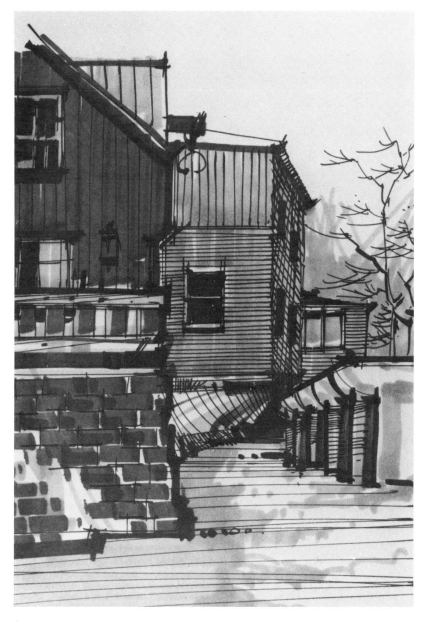

Title: Quechee Lake, Vermont
Original size: 9 x 12 inches
Medium: gray and black markers on
bristol board
Technique: line drawing filled in with
gray markers

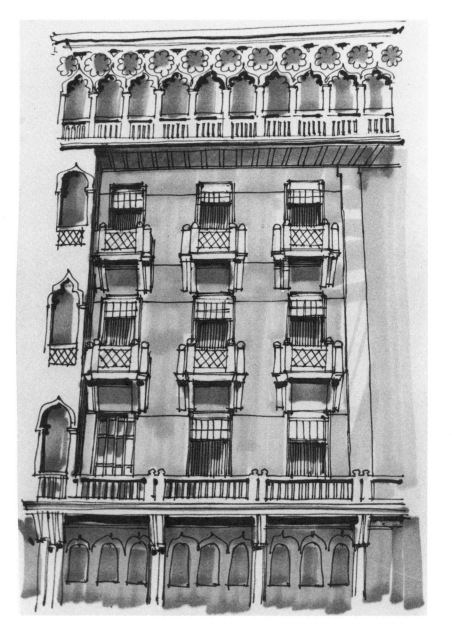

Title: House in Alexandria, Egypt
Original size: 8½ x 11 inches
Medium: Pilot razor point on bristol board,
shading in gray marker
Technique: line and tone drawing

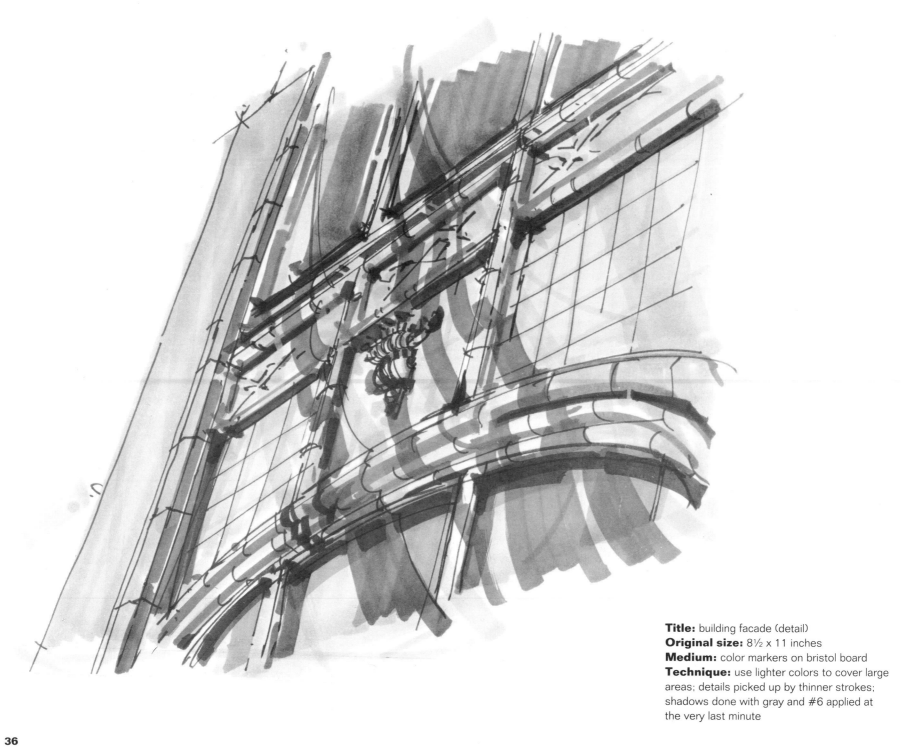

Title: building facade (detail)
Original size: 8½ x 11 inches
Medium: color markers on bristol board
Technique: use lighter colors to cover large areas; details picked up by thinner strokes; shadows done with gray and #6 applied at the very last minute

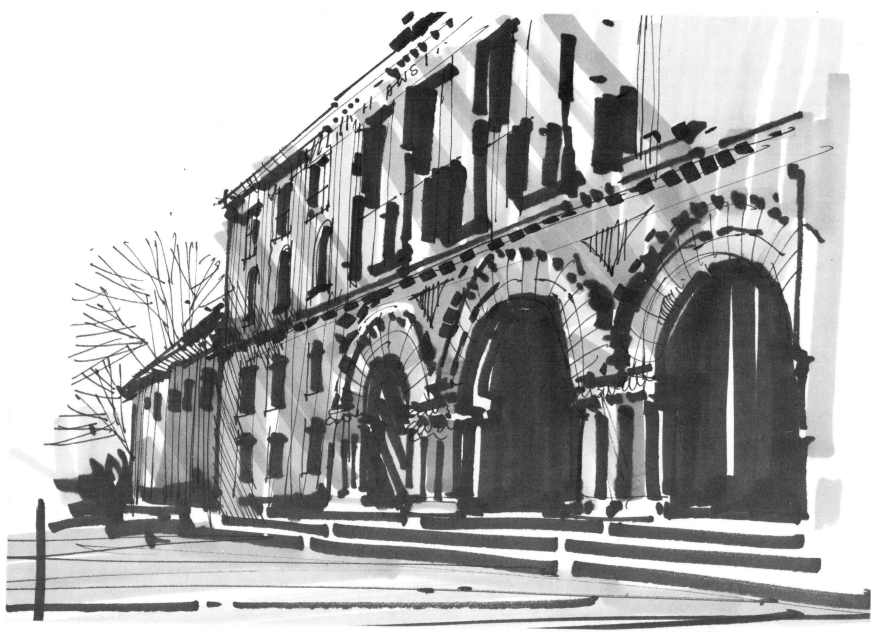

Title: Austin Hall, Harvard University
Original size: 8½ x 11 inches
Medium: black and gray markers on felt-tip-marker paper
Technique: outlining done with Pilot fine-point

Selection of Color Markers

Color choices of markers are ever increasing. It is indeed difficult to start a useful collection because of the many variations of styles and colors and because of the cost factor. You should choose colors according to basic need rather than on impulse. Look for colors that blend well with each other instead of setting up a kaleidoscopic selection. Limit your selection to not more than fifteen or twenty markers. You can always add to your collection as you progress. To ensure intelligent and practical choices, there are three major criteria for consideration. The first is color. There are three separate but closely related functions of color:

- Prime colors (base colors) are used to cover a large area, such as vegetation, architecture, water, or sky. They should be soft and warm and should be able to blend well with all the adjacent colors.
- Supporting colors enhance prime colors. They are used for textural buildup, shading, and edge sharpening.
- Accent colors are for highlighting. They are usually bright, attractive and contradictory. They are often used for cars, signs, clothing, and the like. The location of these colors should be carefully selected: don't overdo them. Since the area of coverage is relatively small, pointed-nib markers are more suitable than wide-nib markers.

The second criterion for marker selection is function. Markers come in different nib sizes and materials. A soft felt tip produces a broad and even stroke while a hard nylon tip produces a thin and consistent streak. The broad and soft nib markers are ideal for filling in large areas, while narrow tips are suited for line and texture drawing. Lines define spatial edges and clarify objects in space. It suggests volume and clarifies depth. The decision here lies in the subject matter and the type of artistic expression that the artist seeks to communicate through his/her sketch.

The last selection criterion involves convenience. This category has less direct impact on the quality of the sketch but nonetheless affects the sketching act. Here are some considerations: the design of the cap and the ease of recapping the marker properly; the shape of the cartridge to prevent the marker from rolling off an inclined surface; the shape, sizes, and weight of the markers and the ease of carrying them to the field; the durability of the nib to stay sharp; smell, fume, and safety concerns; and perhaps cost and affordability. Many of these factors are so trivial and personal that they are matters of individual preference.

In conclusion, the choice of markers should never become a burden that may take the fun away from this creative activity called sketching. To enjoy sketching, the choice of what kinds of marker to buy should be flexible and spontaneous.

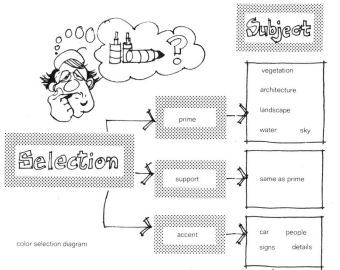

color selection diagram

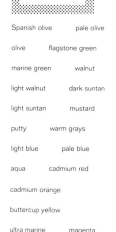

Subject		colors	
vegetation		Spanish olive	pale olive
architecture		olive	flagstone green
landscape		marine green	walnut
water	sky	light walnut	dark suntan
		light suntan	mustard
same as prime		putty	warm grays
		light blue	pale blue
		aqua	cadmium red
car	people	cadmium orange	
signs	details	buttercup yellow	
		ultra marine	magenta

prime — support — accent

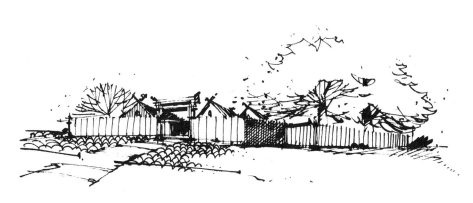

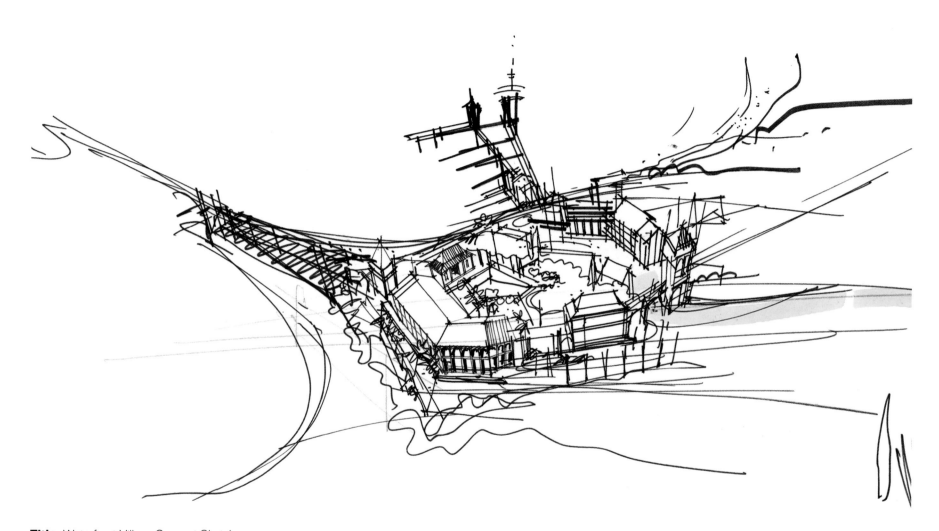

Title: Waterfront Village Concept Sketch

Lay out the composition with bold and fluid strokes, sketch in the individual element, refine and straighten all spatial edges with repeated lines, identify the direction of light source, and begin to highlight the sun-shade contrast by darkening the shaded sides. You may have to repeat this process several times and on several layers of tracing paper.

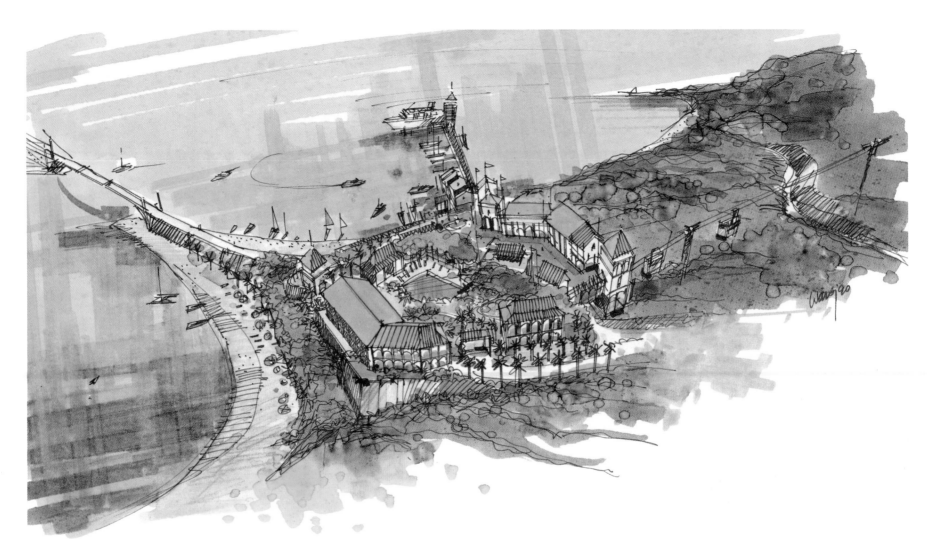

Copy the refined version on good quality
tracing paper. Avoid becoming tense by
maintaining the fluidity of line strokes. Fill in
details as necessary and apply appropriate
colors with markers. Colors that cover large
areas such as ground, water, trees, or sky
should go first. Layer a darker shade of the
same color to achieve a three-dimensional
effect; highlight building roofs and important
spatial edges to bring out the feeling of
depth.

40

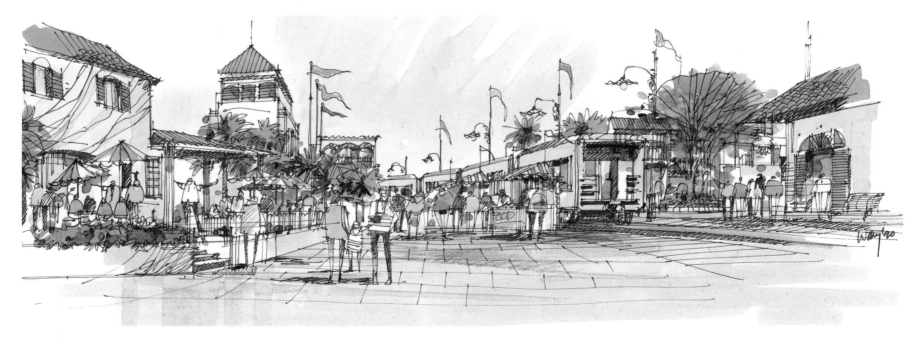

Title: Village Square
Original size: 12 x 20 inches
Medium: color markers on white tracing paper
Technique: color markers on felt-tip sketch

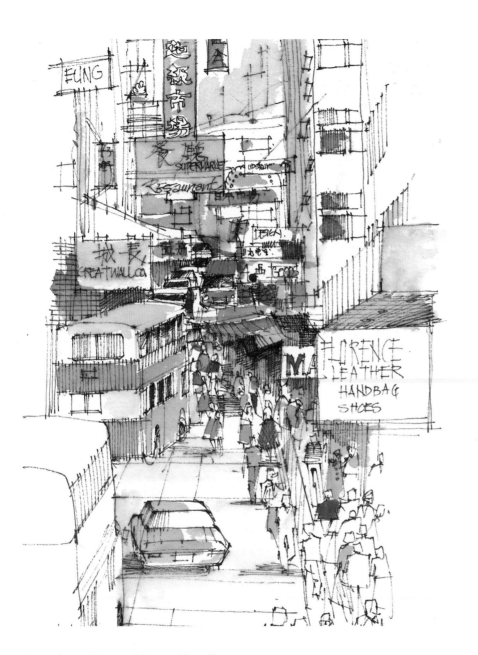

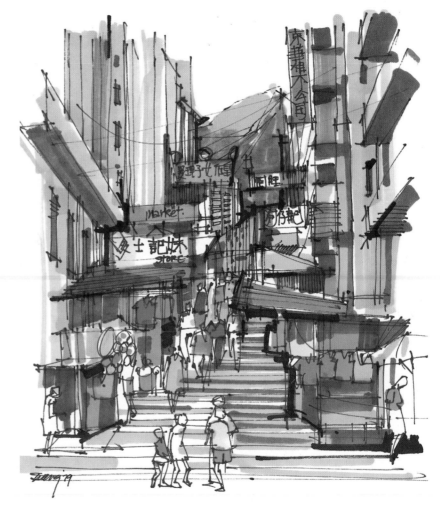

Title: Central District, Victoria, Hong Kong
Original size: 9 x 14 inches
Medium: Pilot fine-line marker and
watercolor wash on watercolor paper
Technique: line drawing and wash

Title: Central District, Victoria, Hong Kong
Original size: 11 x 14 inches
Medium: color markers on Aquabee
felt-tip-marker paper
Technique: line drawing; some spatial
edges defined by broad marker strokes

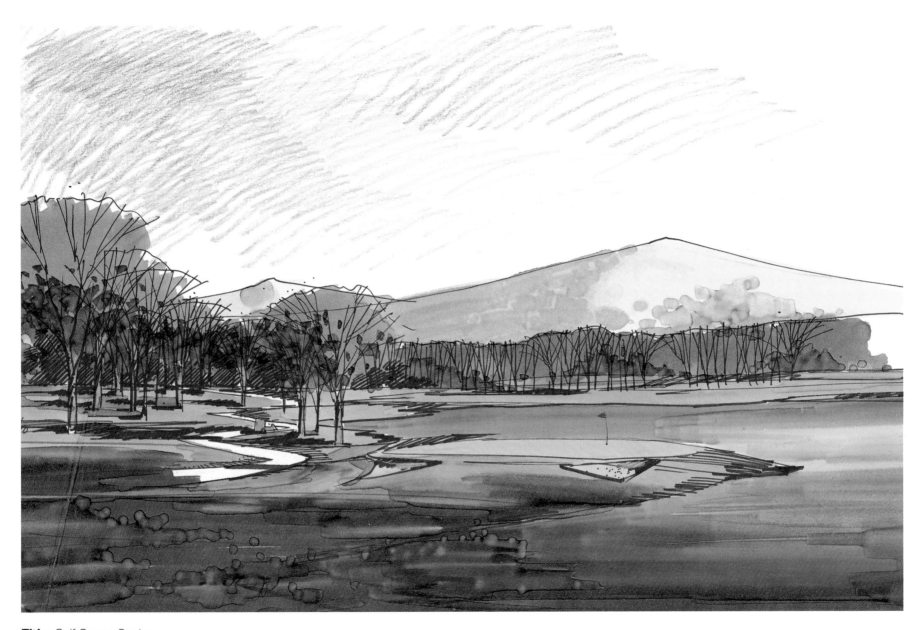

Title: Golf Course Study
Original size: 12 x 20 inches
Medium: color markers on white
tracing paper
Technique: color markers over
felt-tip line sketch

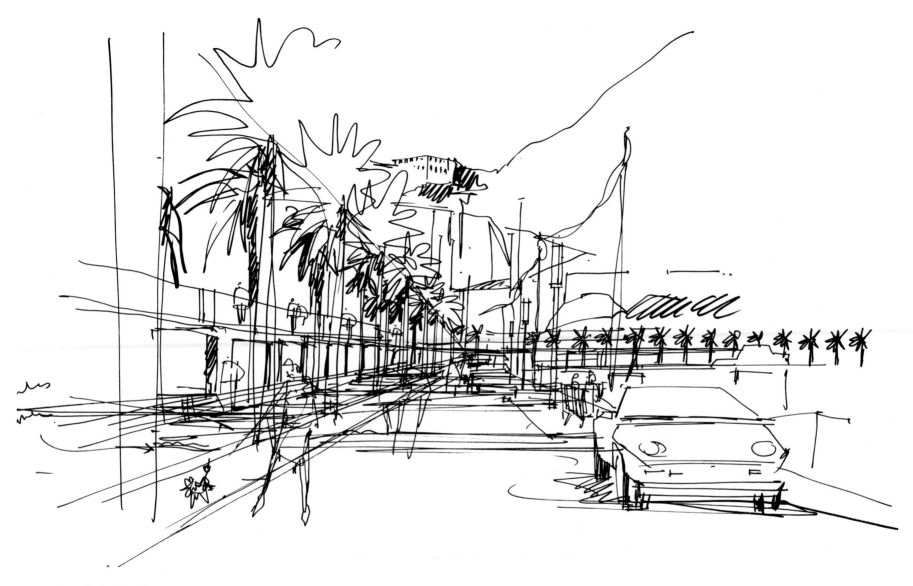

Title: Monte Carlo Waterfront

Establish the horizon line and locate the vanishing point; rough out the location and directions of the projection lines by pulling them out from the vanishing point. Sketch in the composition by quick and loose strokes; use a vertical reference plane such as the building on the left to establish scale. You may have to test several layouts and compositions to get the proper feeling of an accurate perspective.

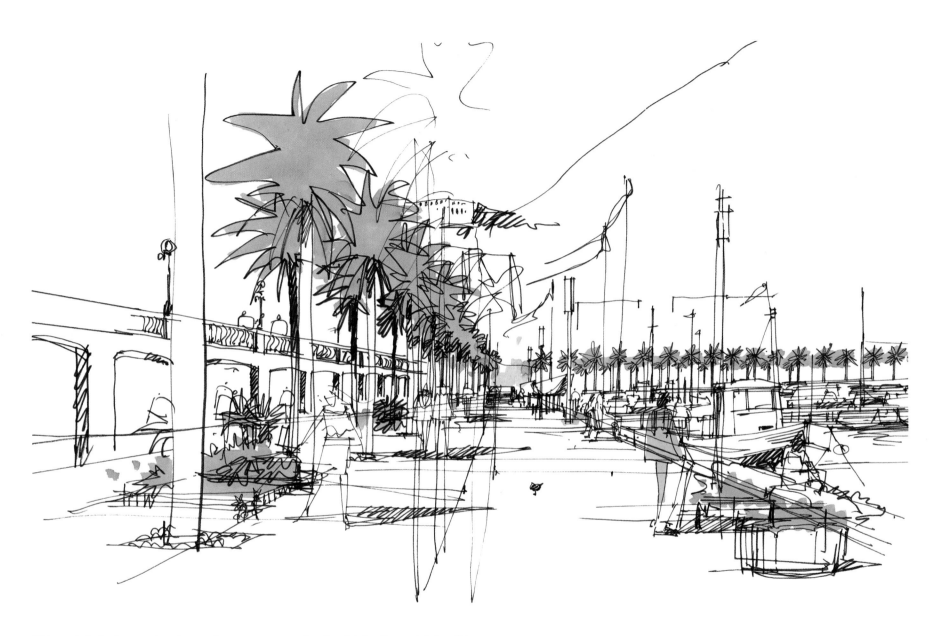

Fill in scale indicators such as human figures, cars, light poles, etc. to get a sense of the proper scale and volume. Use these elements to test the accuracy of the dimension and projection. Delete items that are not satisfactory and continue to fill in and refine the details. These details will increase the degree of realism in the sketch. Use shadows as an anchoring device to stabilize the ground plane. Test the light-shade relationship with color markers.

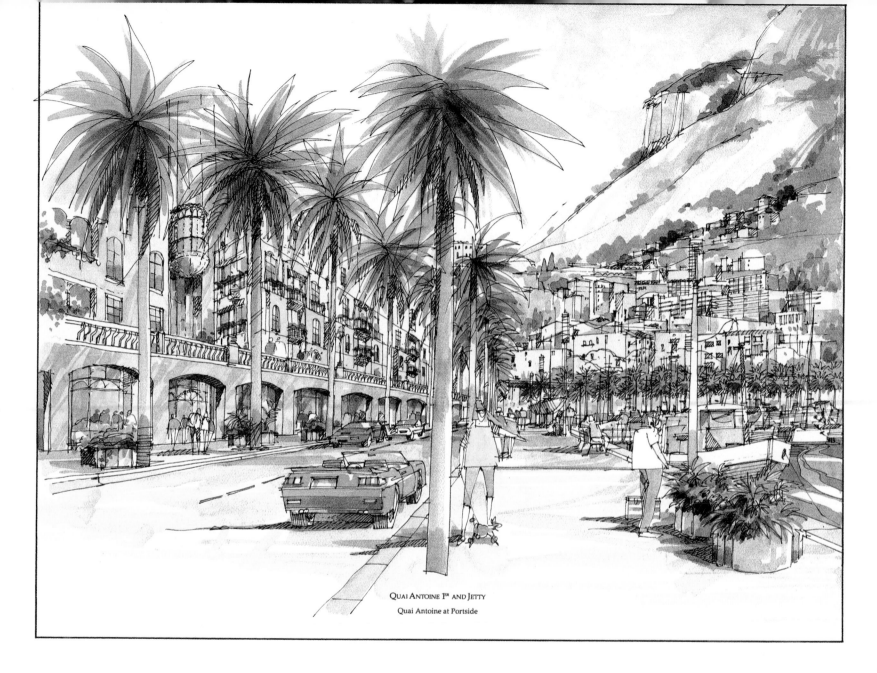

QUAI ANTOINE IER AND JETTY

Quai Antoine at Portside

The final sketch is a traced-line drawing that is machine-copied onto watercolor paper using the large-format photocopying process. The printed image is smudge and waterproofed and is an ideal surface for watercolor application. To prevent the paper from wrapping and buckling during the coloring process, premount it on a rigid styrofoam board. Watercolor is applied in layers to achieve the effect.

SPECIAL TECHNIQUES

Mixing Colors

One of the most intriguing techniques in marker sketching is called mixing, or blending. It takes advantage of the transparent nature of markers by blending different colors one on top of the other to create new colors and to produce new effects. For example, mixing and blending different shades of green on a tree canopy produces a more realistic appearance. Likewise, lighter spots on dark blue water tend to capture the sparkles and reflective nature of the water's surface. Plain marker strokes can look flat and dull when applied evenly, but mixing and blending will bring out the three-dimensional quality of the sketch.

However, this process can be risky, with often unpredictable results that are difficult to control. The risk lies in the unpredictability. Since mixing is often done halfway into the sketching process, errors of this kind are irreversible and can jeopardize the entire sketch. The only and most effective way to learn this technique is by trial and error, through which one can learn predictable patterns and results by testing and mixing different colors. Keep in mind that different brands of markers and different types of papers also produce different results.

To mix colors, you should be familiar with the color wheel and the nature of color. For example, red mixed with yellow produces orange, and blue mixed with yellow produces green. However, due to the chemical content and the rate at which the marker dries on a particular surface, yellow on red may be different from red on yellow. Again, one must pre-test to become familiar with this kind of reaction. In addition, the markers used in mixing will no longer retain their original color due to contamination on their felt tips. They should be stored separately and labelled for easy identification.

To create the "bleeding" effect of watercolor, systematically place selective colors on top of the original layer to dilute the original color while it is drying. For a more dynamic result, the wet on wet technique is very effective. To achieve maximum results, layer lighter colors on top of darker ones. Though not absolute, the reversal of this process often leads to a dark, muddy effect.

To achieve a satisfactory mixing result, a slow-drying drawing surface is required. White tracing paper is an excellent medium for test-mixing markers. It does not absorb quickly and it dries relatively slowly. The colors remain brilliant and true. Another excellent medium is photographic paper. The special coating is an ideal surface for mixing and blending, and colors are erasable. However, this special plastic coating tends to lighten the overall color effect. Another drawback with photographic paper is cost. It is very expensive! One should try to avoid any kind of bonded papers made from fibres. This includes watercolor paper, bristol paper, and any paper stocks that have a high absorption rate.

Use lighter fluid—such as Bestine—to erase markers, or a regular white eraser on photographic paper. To erase a large area, a few drops of rubber cement solvent on a dinner napkin pick up and clean a large area. Bear in mind that the type of paper and the coating on the drawing surface dictates the effectiveness of erasing.

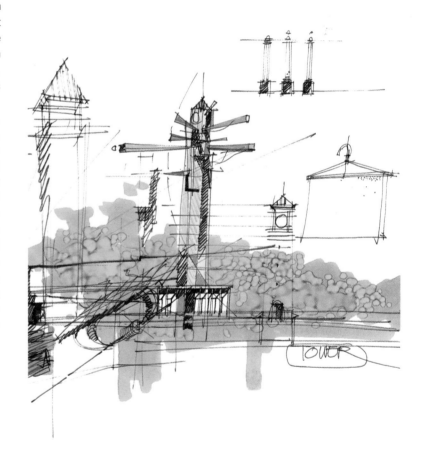

Title: Architectural Study
Original size: 12 x 8 inches
Medium: markers and colored pencils
Technique: mixing of markers

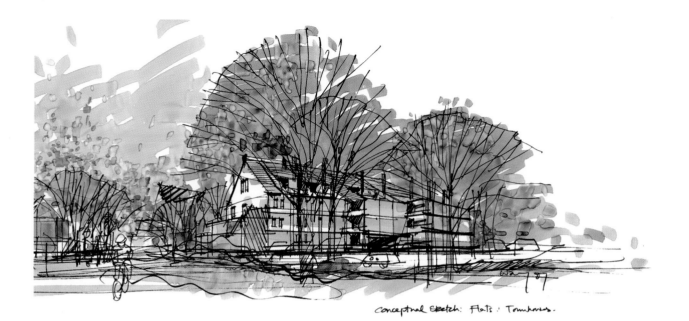

Conceptual Sketch: Flats : Townhouses.

Title: Housing Study
Original size: 14 x 18 inches
Medium: markers on photographic paper
Technique: quick sketch

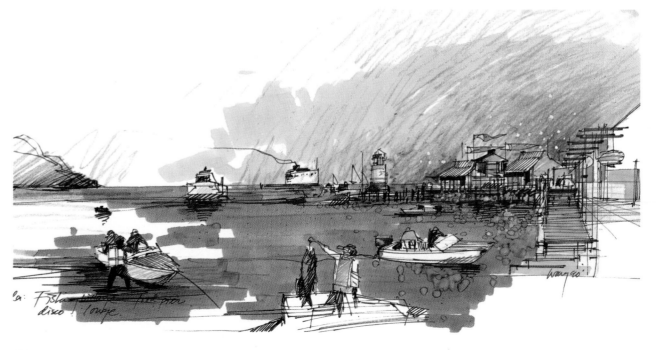

Title: Waterfront Market
Original size: 12 x 18 inches
Medium: color markers on white tracing paper
Technique: color markers on felt-tip line sketch; some mixing and color pencils on sky

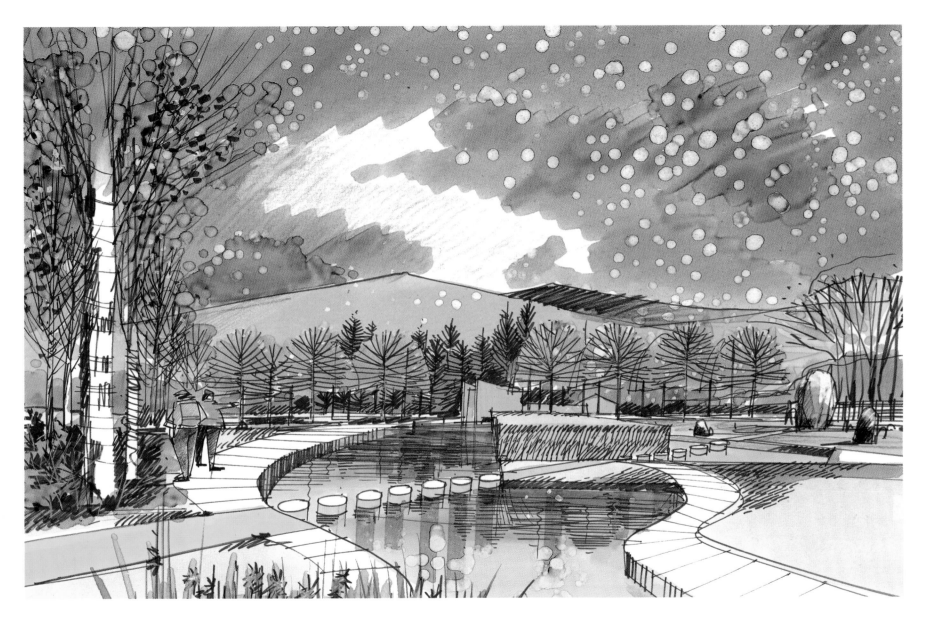

Title: Fountain Study
Original size: 12 x 12 inches
Medium: felt-tip marker and colored pencil
on white tracing paper
Technique: quick sketch, with lighter fluid
drops to create the effect of snowfall.

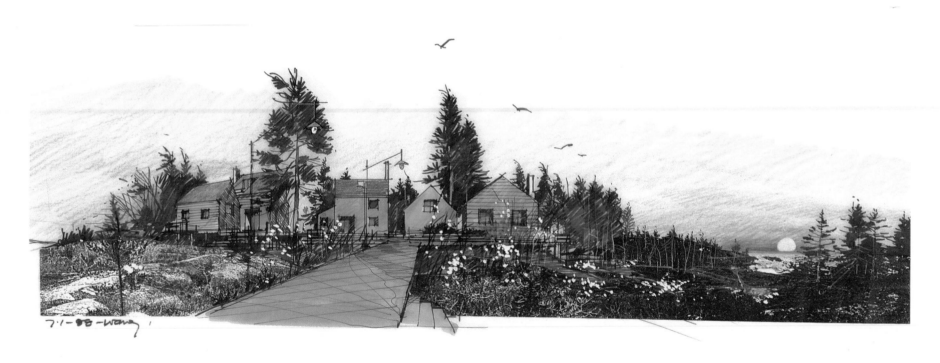

Title: Architectural Study
Original size: 18 x 30 inches
Medium: felt-tip markers, colored pencil
on white tracing paper
Technique: sketch and photographic
montage

Markers and Pencils

The beauty of a sketch done with color marker lies in the brilliancy and transparency of colors. The bold marker strokes and the broad coverage all become parts of the unique "marker style." However, this kind of coverage tends to produce a relatively flat appearance and lacks fine grain and textural effect. Color pencils compensate for this deficiency. The strokes from color pencils and their deliberate directions become the counterpoint to the flat marker streaks. Pencils add sparkle and fizz to the sketch. The overall effect is refreshing and relieves boredom.

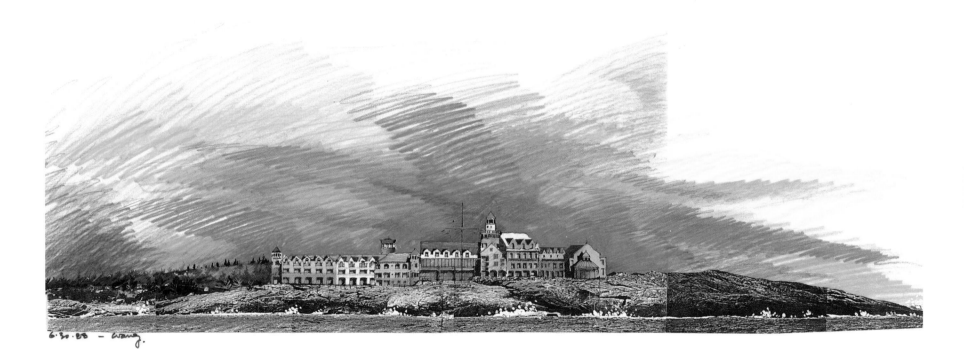

Title: Architectural Study
Original size: 18 x 30 inches
Medium: felt-tip markers, colored pencil on white tracing paper
Technique: sketch and photographic montage

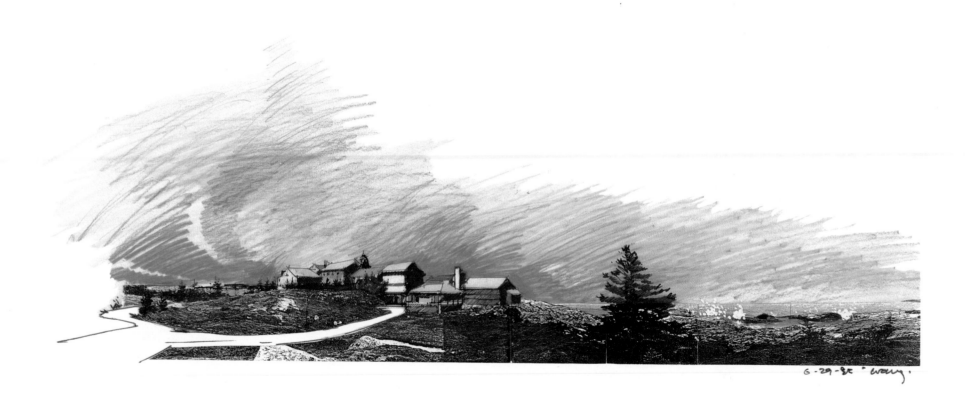

Title: Architectural Study
Original size: 18 x 30 inches
Medium: felt-tip markers, colored pencil
on white tracing paper
Technique: sketch and photographic
montage

Markers and Watercolor

Although the effect of marker sketching is quite similar to that of watercolor, the two media are actually quite different in nature and application. Markers strive for instant effect. The colors are premixed and come ready to use. The result is bright, loud, and perhaps pungent both to the eyes and the nose. On the other hand, watercolor must be mixed; it takes time to achieve the desired effect; it is light, quiet, and reserved. However, despite the differences in style and personality between these two media, watercolor and markers can complement and support each other. Markers are used routinely to supplement watercolor and to increase the intensity of its color effect. Fine-line markers are often used instead of ink pen to create the line-drawing base for watercolor application.

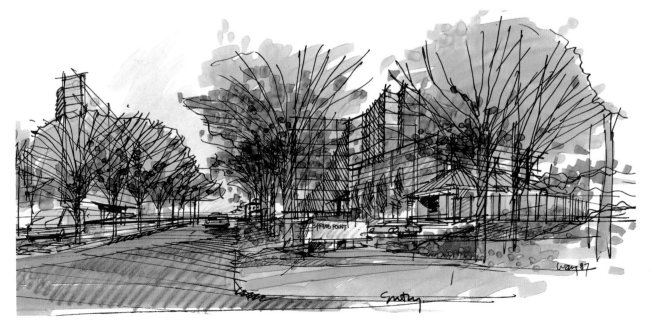

Title: Housing Study
Original size: 14 x 18 inches
Medium: color markers on photographic paper
Technique: quick line drawing on tracing paper before copying photographically; mixing of markers

53

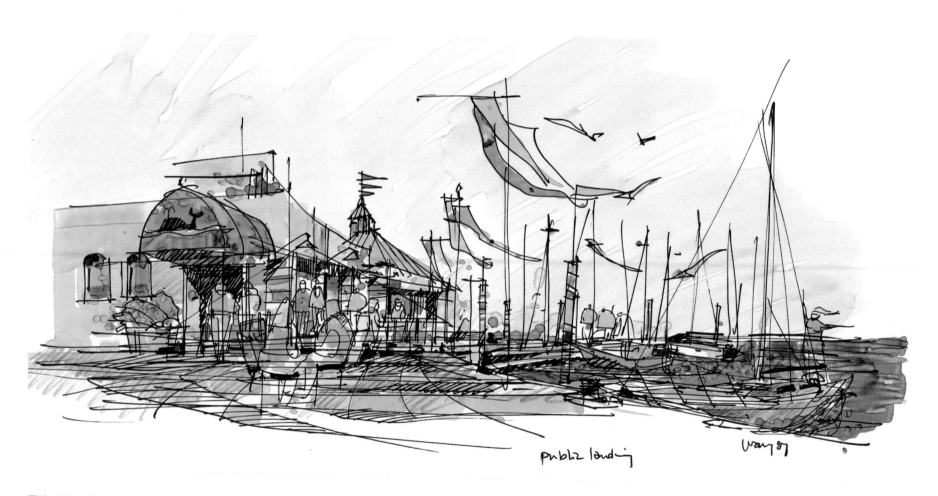

public landing

Title: Waterfront Market
Original size: 14 x 18 inches
Medium: color markers on photographic
paper
Technique: quick line drawing on tracing
paper before copying photographically; mixing
of markers as well as color pencil on sky

Use of Gray Markers

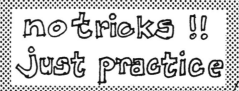

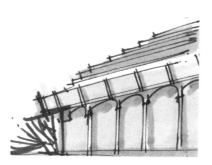

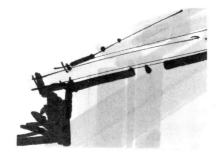

diagonal strokes over vertical strokes create
uneven shadow pattern

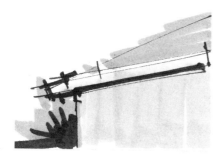

parallel strokes (roof and wall)

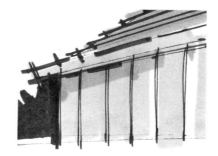

spatial edges outlined and sharp-
ened by fine-line marker, wall
detail also shown

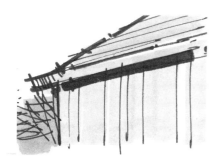

gray marker for base color, spatial edges
outlined by fine-line marker

roof and wall details revealed, darker gray
used to cast shadow

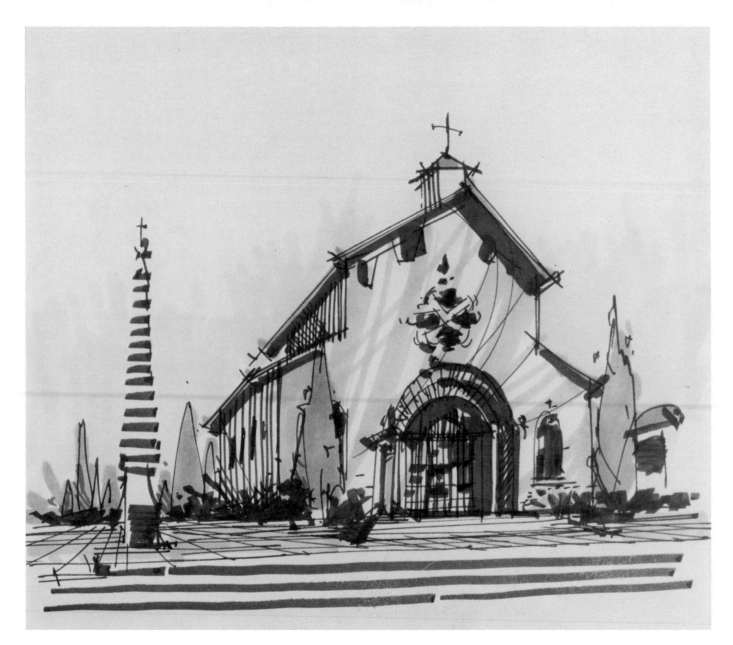

Title: Church in Altos de Chavon,
The Dominican Republic
Original size: 8½ x 11 inches
Medium: color markers on bristol board
Technique: use broad color strokes to
define masses; thin black outlines done
at the last minute

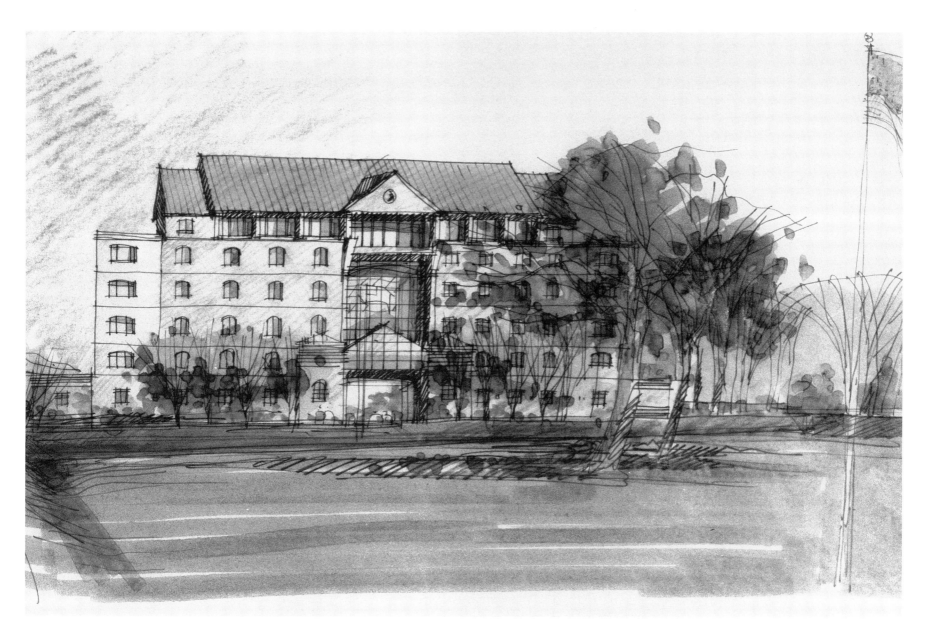

Title: Architectural Study
Original size: 30 x 36 inches
Medium: color markers and felt-tip markers
on white tracing paper
Technique: quick sketch, color markers
over felt-tip line sketch

SKETCHING

Sketching is an artistic act. There are two types of sketching: life drawing, (i.e., you sketch what you see) or recall sketching (i.e., sketching from memory). Sketching is a very complicated interactive process between the eyes and the hands. In the course of transforming real images into symbols, one goes through three distinct stages: object identification, shape simplification, and finally image recording. Keep in mind that this is an oversimplified analysis of the sketching process. What really goes on in your mind and how you graphically express an image are complex and beyond our understanding. Sketching is a gradual learning process. You must learn how to draw before you can sketch. It is like learning how to walk before you can run. Being able to draw precisely, carefully, and realistically is a necessary discipline before attempting

the more difficult task of graphic shorthand. Life drawing, therefore, is a prerequisite skill that enables you to learn how to draw precisely.

Life drawing sets up the fundamentals of sketching. It is an exercise for your eyes, hands, and the entire linkage system. Life drawing not only lets you study the object with your eyes, it sometimes involves taking real measurement of the dimensions and angles, or recording the materials and textures with photographs. These routines habitually force your eyes to keenly record the image and, therefore, remember it. The fact that you remember the image is crucial to sketching from recollection or memory. Often you cannot recall images because you don't have them in your visual data bank. The idea that we can't draw often derives from the lack of anything to recall. It is not a matter of skill.

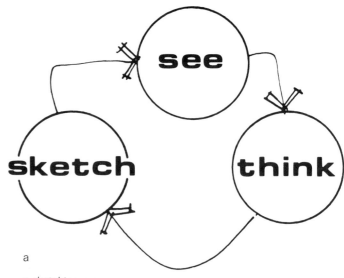

a

a sketching process

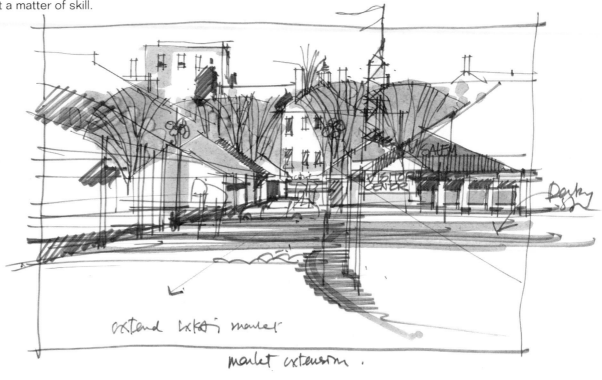

Title: Urban Space Study
Original size: 8 x 11 inches
Medium: markers on white tracing paper
Technique: quick sketch

b

SEEING

Since sketching records visual experience, the art of seeing and the things we see are indeed the crucial factors in sketching.

Learning to see is the most important step in learning about life drawing. Since the sketching process records visual experience, the art of seeing and the things we see are indeed crucial factors.

Most of our visual experiences have to do with a perceived message. People endow the objects they see with a certain meaning, which is factual and utilitarian. For example, observers may identify a door as a door that leads to a restaurant; a house, as a courthouse. Seeing in sketching should precede such facts. First of all, you should be aware of the juxtapositioning of objects, the changing of colors, the variation in contour and light quality, and the liveliness of lines and edges. Before interpreting the meaning of the things you see, first appreciate the proportion, scale, texture, and composition of the entire image. This is called aesthetic seeing, or formal perception.

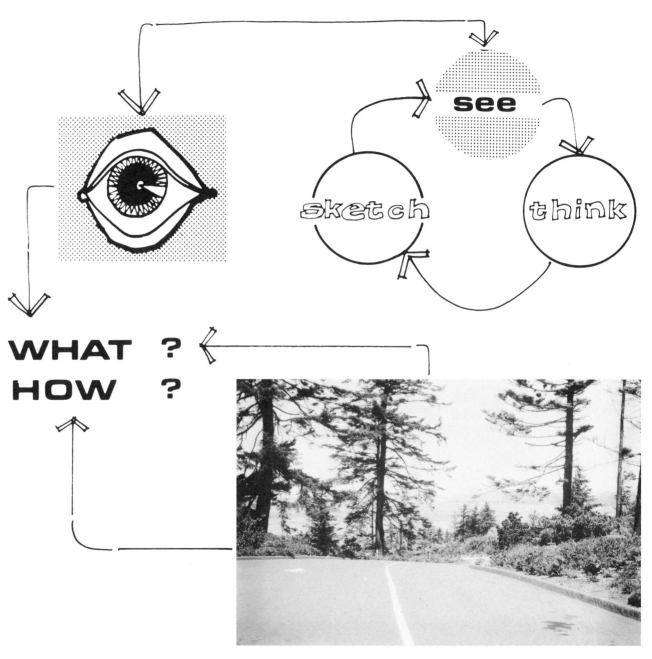

WHAT ?
HOW ?

The Art of Seeing

Kevin Lynch, in his book *Image of the City* (MIT Press, 1961), described edges, landmarks, nodes, and paths as the prime visual attractions of the city. Seeing in sketching is quite similar. The three major categories in formal perception are:

- Skyline—look for the mass, landmarks, nodes, and figure/ground relationship (Figure a).
- Light/shade contrast—identify the light source, as it helps to pictorialize the shape of the masses (Figure b).
- Lines, paths, and edges—these help to identify perspective and locate reference planes and vanishing points (Figure c).

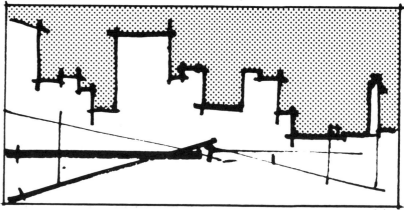

a   profile, figure/ground relationship

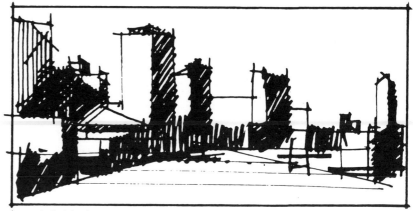

b   light/shade contrast, shape identification

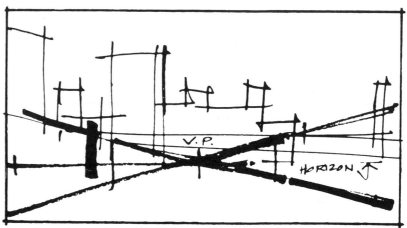

c   line, edge, and perspective

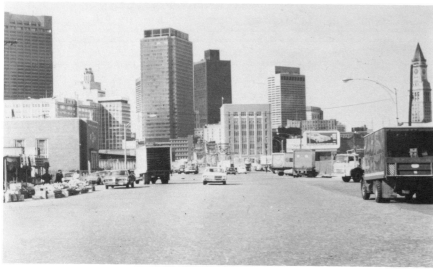

photograph of a city

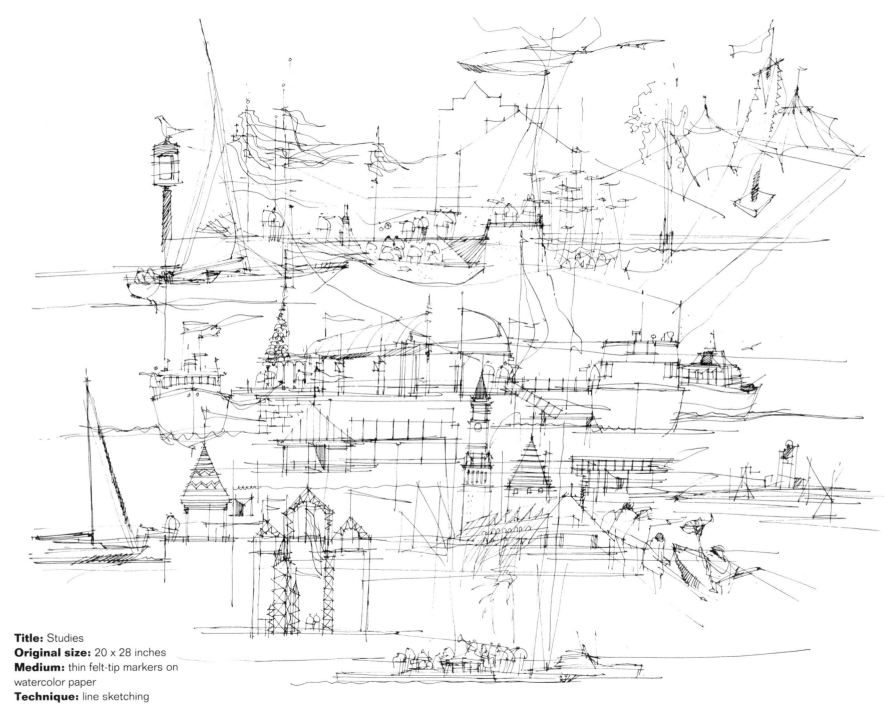

Title: Studies
Original size: 20 x 28 inches
Medium: thin felt-tip markers on
watercolor paper
Technique: line sketching

SEEING METHODS

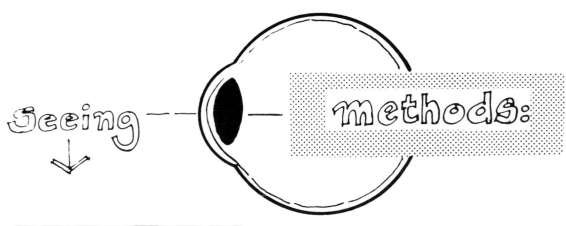 Seeing → methods:

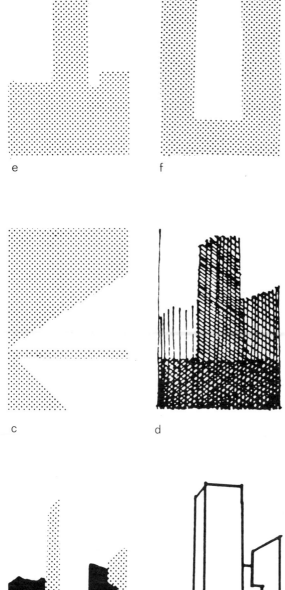

e   f

c   d

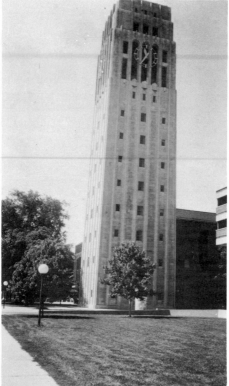

Here are several suggestions for aesthetic observation:

- Differentiate the figure/ground relationship and understand the proportion between mass and space (Figure a).
- Identify the prominent mass and its coverage inside the picture frame (Figure b).
- Identify the perspective type and locate the horizon line, projection rays, and reference planes (Figure c).
- Classify the visual field into foreground, middleground, and background. (Figure d).
- Identify the light source and sketch out the tonal contrast of the major planes (Figure e).
- Identify the shape of masses by following the formative lines (horizontal, vertical, and diagonal) (Figure f).

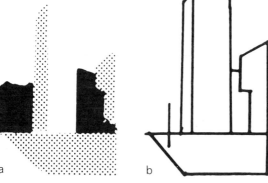

a   b

One-point Perspective

One of the most important aspects of seeing is understanding the perspective type and structure of the scene. They are the foundation of all measurement, and they determine the proportion and scale of the sketch. Correct perspective is the skeleton of a good sketch. Perspective does not yield a duplicate of the perceived image, but it comes closest to, or best explains, our perceptual experience.

Normally, when we face an object (e.g., Figure a), our line of vision is perpendicular to the frontal or portal plane. In Figure a the frontal plane is a hypothetical plane, and the portal plane is the rear wall and stained-glass window. The reference planes (floor, wall, columns, etc.) and projection lines are parallel to the center of vision. Due to the nature of one-point perspective, these lines tend to look as if they are converging at a distant point located on the horizon (eye level) (Figure b).

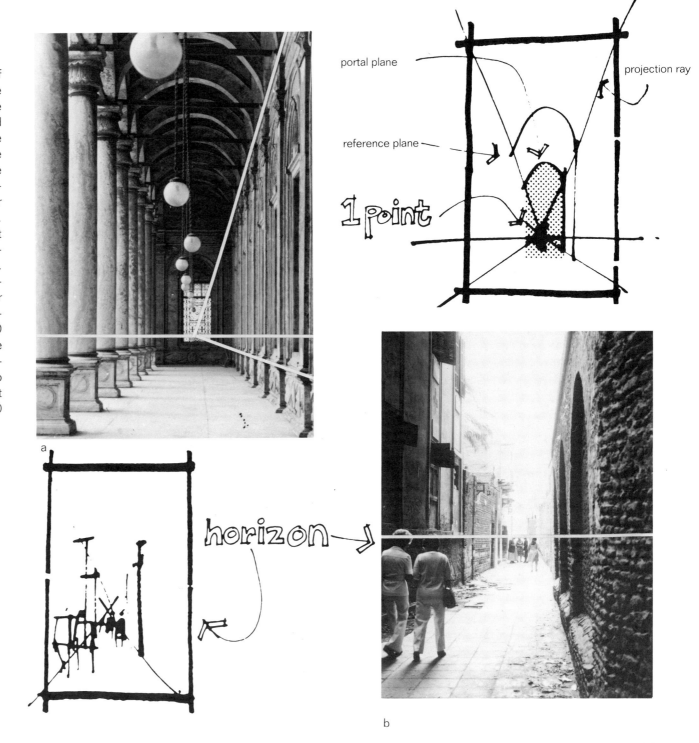

portal plane

projection ray

reference plane

1 point

a

horizon →

b

63

Perceptual Interpretation

According to Erwin Panofsky (*Studies in Iconology, Humanistic Themes in the Art of the Renaissance*, Icon Editions, 1972), there are two major ways of interpreting perceptual experience: in terms of either formal or factual meaning.

Formal perception is a conglomerate of certain patterns of color, line, and volume that constitutes an image. It captures the silhouette of the image and carries no specific meaning or message. This *experience* takes place during the first instant of an entire perceptual sequence. It is followed immediately by factual perception, during which the viewer begins to understand the experience. Factual perception involves identifying certain visible objects known from previous experience, as well as relationships between these objects and cues within the image. Its meaning is often unique to a given culture.

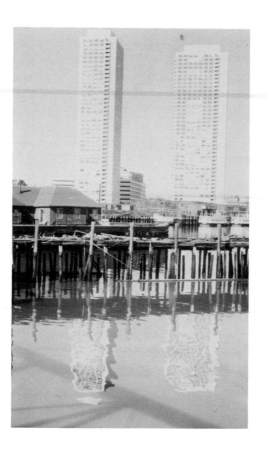

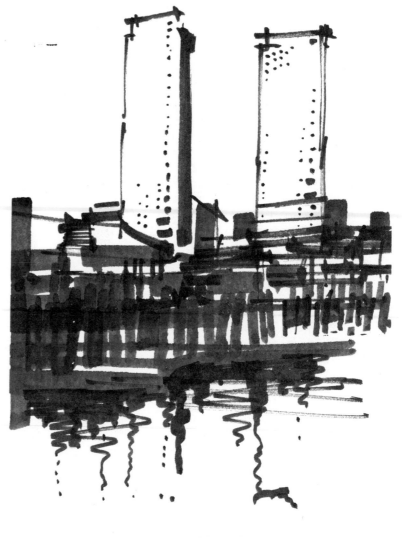

Formal perception can be subdivided into four parts: mass, line, shape, and tone. Mass refers to the figure/ground relationship. It separates the object (mass) from the space (ground). It categorically groups objects that share similar features without differentiating materials, details, and intervening spatial edges (Figure b). Line concerns the predominant orientation(s) of the major structures (Figure c). Shape expresses the character of each object within the picture frame (Figure d), while tone identifies the logical light source and creates the sensation of depth (Figure e).

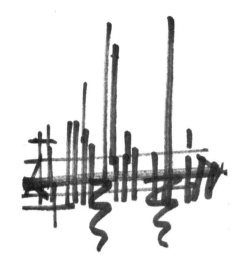

b

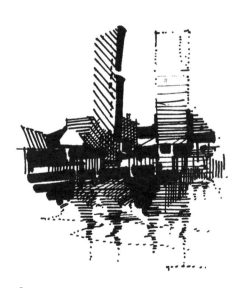

c

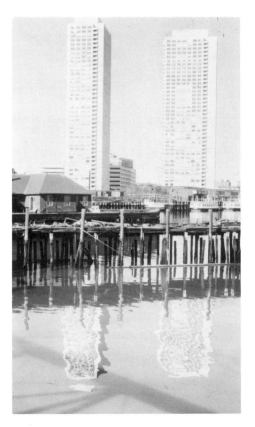

a

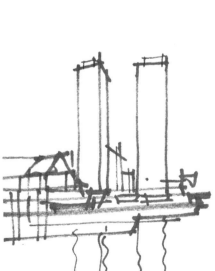

d

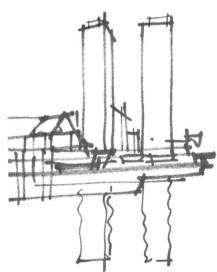

e

65

Composition of Identifiable Units

The secondary level of visual interpretation involves subject matter and meaning. These are identifiable components of the image and are located in all three levels of our visual field: foreground, middleground, and background. The position of the viewer determines the degree of complexity of the image and the extent of juxtapositioning. It also determines the size of the picture and controls the perspective. It is important to learn how to see these components as individual units as well as a totality. The ability to dissect a scene visually and put it back together in a simplified fashion is the key to the technique of sketching.

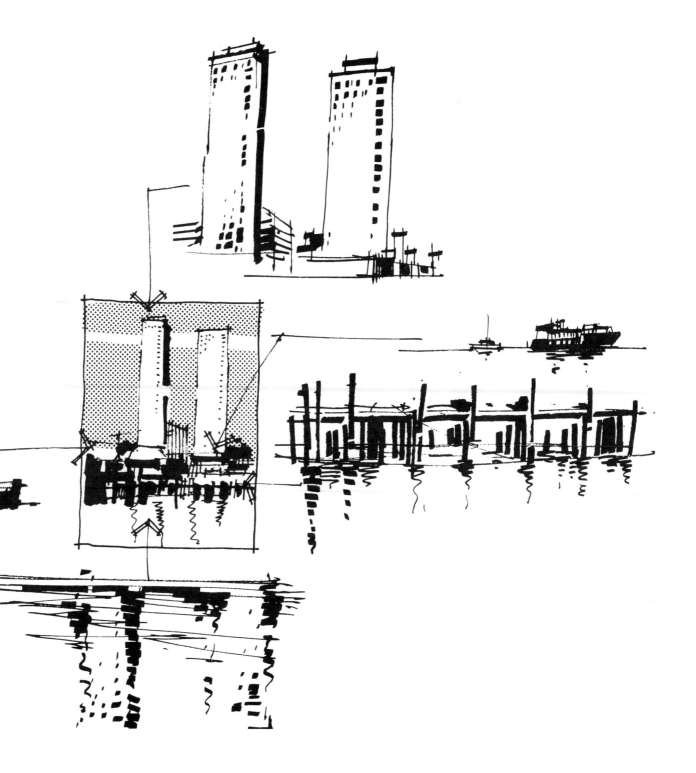

Two-point Perspective

Two-point perspectives differ from one-point perspectives in the disappearance of the frontal plane. The viewer has a better vantage point and can see more of and understand better the structure of the image. However, due to the setup of the perspective and the facts that the rate of scale change and size diminishing is greater, the drawing has a greater potential of distortion.

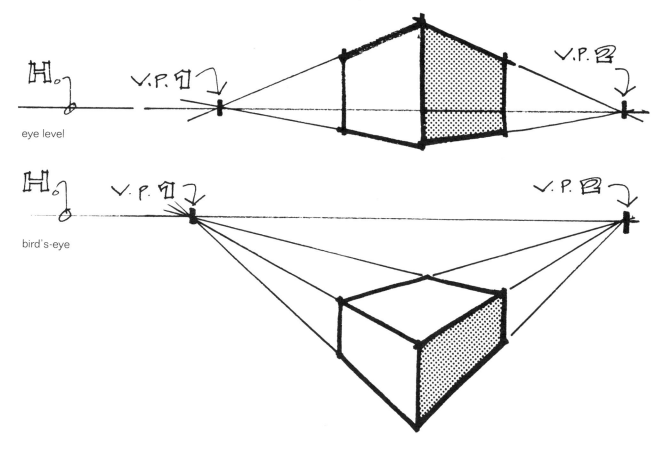

eye level

bird's-eye

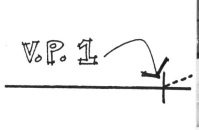

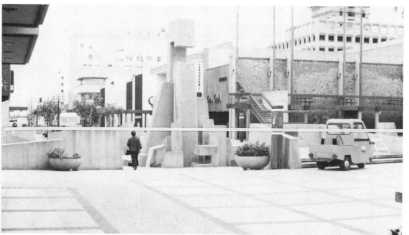

Three-point Perspective

Three-point perspective is a combination of one- and two-point perspectives. It is a spinoff of a one-point perspective because of the horizontal extension of the frontal plane (Figure a). The drawing will be extremely distorted unless the frontal plane is bent. This creates a curved picture plane (frontal plane), which functions as a fisheye or wide-angle lens (Figure b). The purpose is to widen and broaden the coverage, enhancing our normal perceptual experience and minimizing distortion

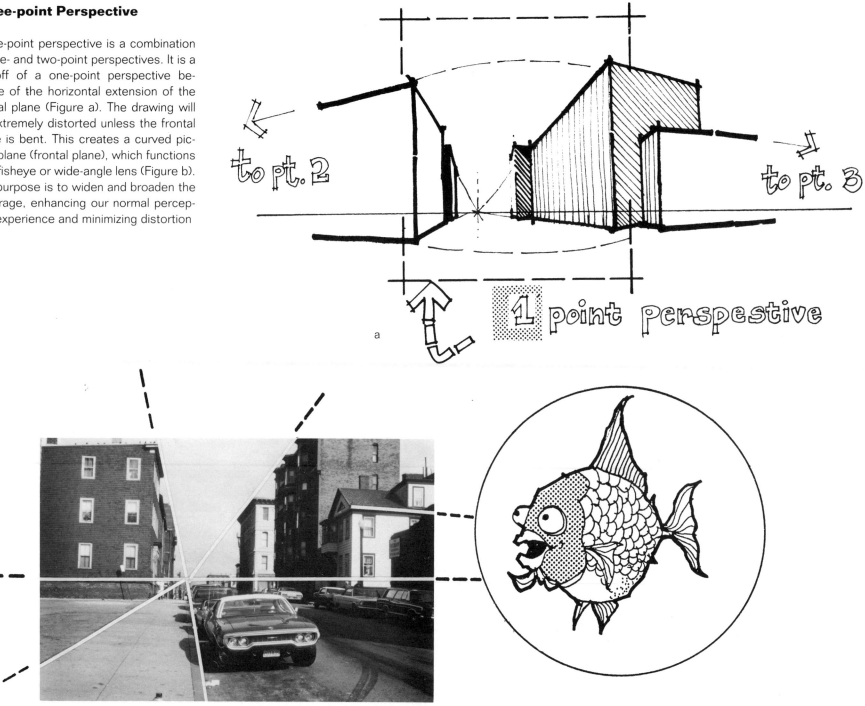

to pt. 2

to pt. 3

1 point Perspestive

a

b

Natural Scenery

When drawing natural scenery, the frontal plane is often nonexistent, because identifiable reference planes established by built elements are not present. Under such circumstances, one should not rely on the reference planes to establish the benchmark for measurement and scale. The best way to sketch in this situation is to outline the edges of the three major visual fields (i.e., those between foreground, middleground, and background). These edges should be bold and heavy, emphasizing only the major profile and outline of the mass and never the detailed serration of individual elements.

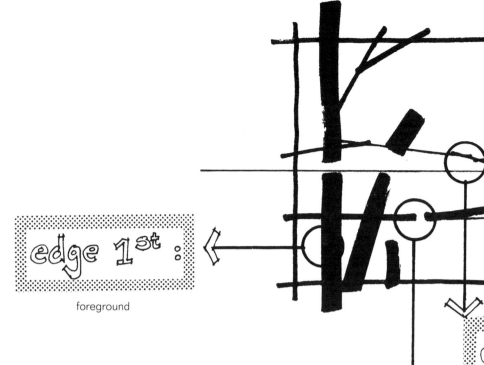

edge 1st :

foreground

edge 3rd :

background

edge 2nd :

middleground

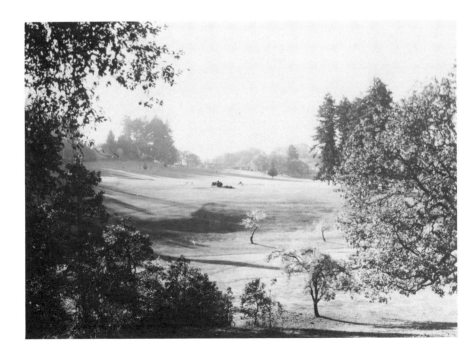

Special Perspective

Bird's-eye views are among the most frequently used perspectives for special effects in sketching. The behavior of the horizontal parallel lines is the same as in ordinary perspectives. However, the vertical parallel lines can be drawn either parallel or converging to a point below (Figure a) or above (Figure b) the horizon line. This shift of parallelism exaggerates the scale and extends the sense of height. This technique is often used to sketch tall objects such as highrises or monuments.

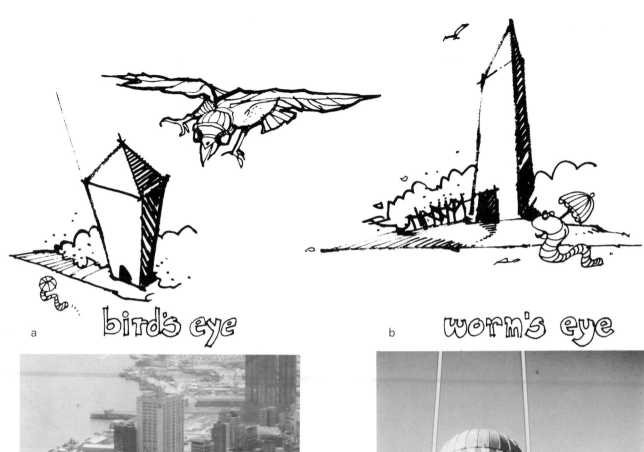

a **bird's eye**

b **worm's eye**

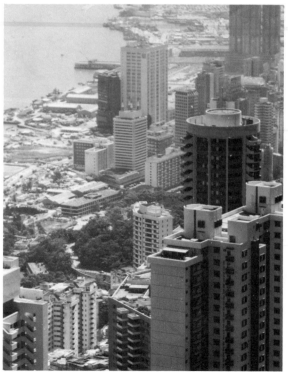

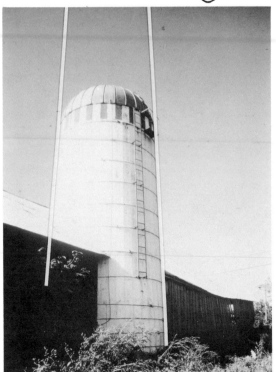

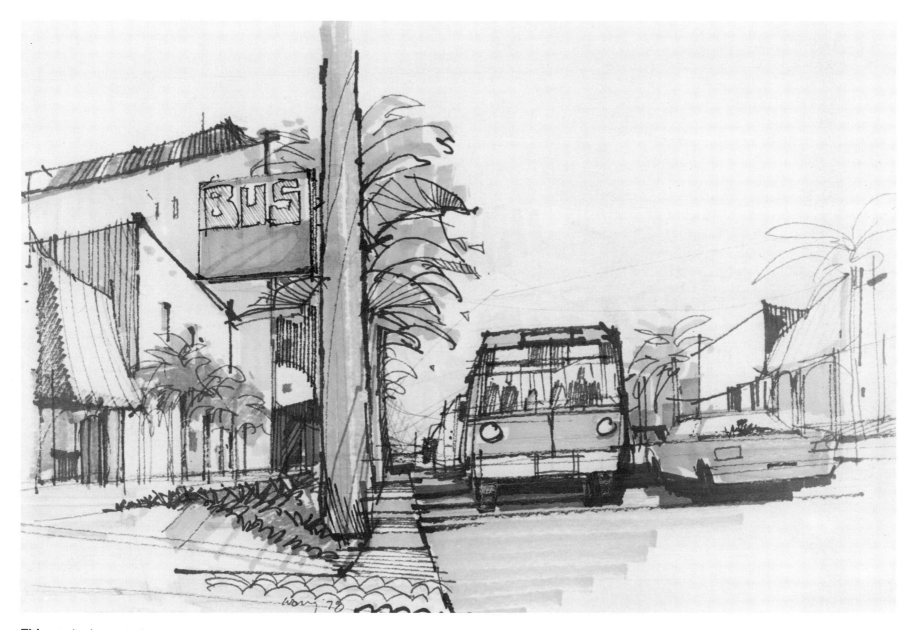

Title: studio demonstration
Original size: 11 x 17 inches
Medium: color markers on watercolor paper
Technique: outlining of spatial edges with
black pentel after the masses were rendered
and filled on broad color

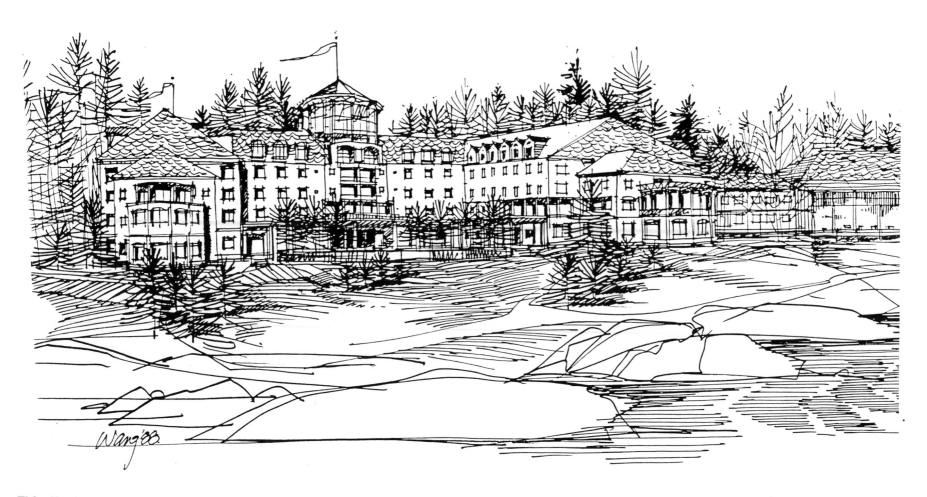

Title: Hotel
Original size: 12 x 20 inches
Medium: markers and color pencil on
yellow tracing paper
Technique: line drawing

Picture Plane

Sketching records a three-dimensional scene onto a two-dimensional surface. Before the image is drawn, it must be temporarily captured on a hypothetical plane called the picture frame. This function is very similar to that of the camera, in which the image is recorded on film in less than a second. The picture frame is used to determine the size of the sketch and the amount of the coverage. It frames those objects that you want to sketch and blocks out the undesirable ones (Figure a). The opening of the picture frame should be proportional to the paper used. Empty slide mounts are very convenient tools for framing purposes. Simply hold the mount in front of you and move it back and forth to determine how much you want to sketch. If the frame is closer to the object, the amount of coverage is reduced and the size of the object is increased. On the other hand, if the frame is closer to you, the amount of coverage increases and the size of objects becomes smaller (Figure b). Most experienced artists bypass this step, not because they think it unnecessary, but because their eyes can automatically do the cropping within the picture frame.

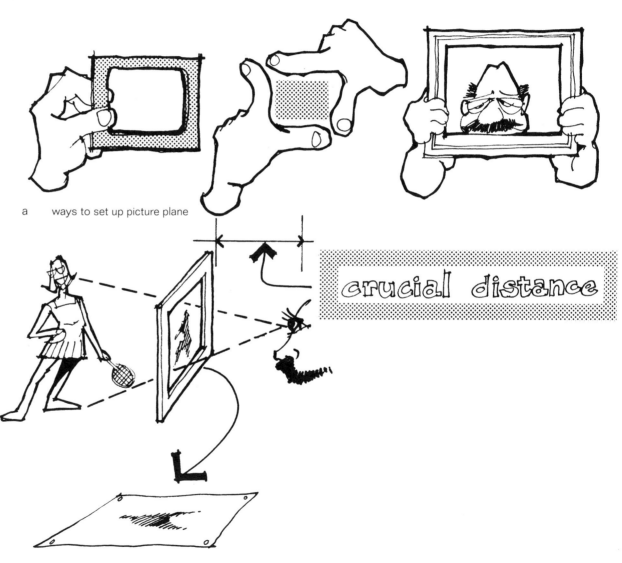

a   ways to set up picture plane

crucial distance

b   position of the picture plane and viewing distance

COMPOSITION

Location of the Horizon

The horizon is the eye level of the artist (viewer). The location of the horizon on the sheet will ultimately determine the location of the principal elements. It will also divide the sheet into two horizontal bands that may or may not complement each other. This horizontal division of the sheet is extremely important in the composition of a sketch.

One should avoid placing the horizon across the center of the page. It divides the sheet into two equal portions and produces a static and boring image. For the most effective composition, place the horizon at either a three-quarter or a one-quarter position. A low horizon (Figure a) has more sky space and tends to emphasize the verticality of objects. A high horizon (Figure b) is ideal for bird's-eye or oblique views. Due to the viewing angle, the depth dimension does not foreshorten as quickly as does a low horizon, so most foreground details must be included.

a

b

Title: Design Study
Original size: 11 x 24 inches
Medium: markers and color pencil on yellow tracing paper
Technique: section sketch, color pencils over felt-tip sketch

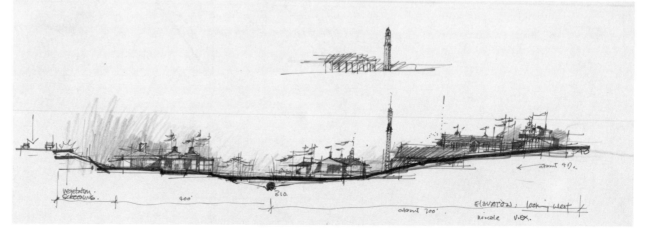

Positioning of the Mass

Arrange the elements in such a manner as to lead the viewer into the picture. Always position the dominant mass away from the center of the page in order to create a sense of false instability. This tends to control the eye movement of the viewer and gives the feeling that the subject is lively and not bound by the edges of the picture. The frame should be looked upon as a temporal mechanism used reluctantly to capture and suspend a moving scene for a split second. The most successful sketch is one that, although bound by the sheet, looks as if it is going to break loose.

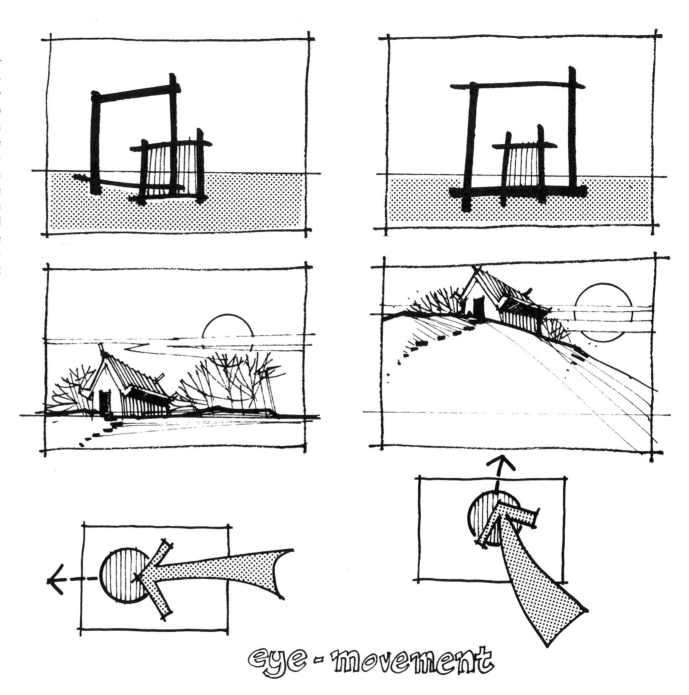

eye - movement

Balance

Avoid symmetrical balance. Shift the viewing position or change the sheet format to create the feeling of occult or asymmetrical balance, which is dynamic and interesting. It employs the juxtapositioning of mass and space to create a perceived but not obvious balance. The mass/space relationship is often contradictory in texture, color, and shape, but the areas should be kept relatively similar. Occult balance has a built-in system and tension and should not be misunderstood as random positioning.

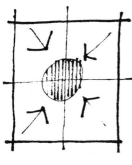

axial balance

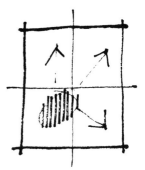

occult balance

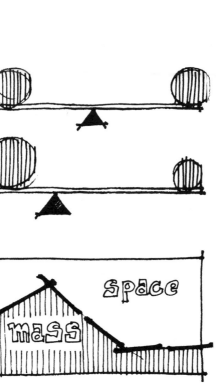

balance between mass and space

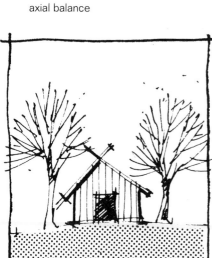

symmetrical layout

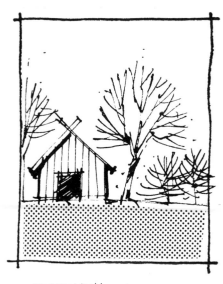

asymmetrical layout

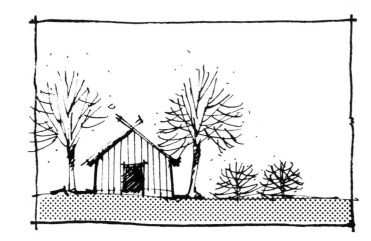

horizontal format

SELECTION OF PERSPECTIVE

One-point Perspective

One-point perspective gives equal exposure to both sides of the lateral dimension (Figure a). Shifting the center of vision creates an uneven exposure (Figure b). This is often done to avoid a symmetrical composition for subjects to which symmetry would not be appropriate. For example, one side of a street may be more important than the other.

One-point perspective is straightforward, and is simple and easy to understand. Such a composition encourages the use of line (streets, trees, etc.) to lead into the subject. It has a strong sense of direction, and it provides an excellent setting for the expression of repetition and rhythm.

One-point perspective is ideal for sketching street scenes and interiors.

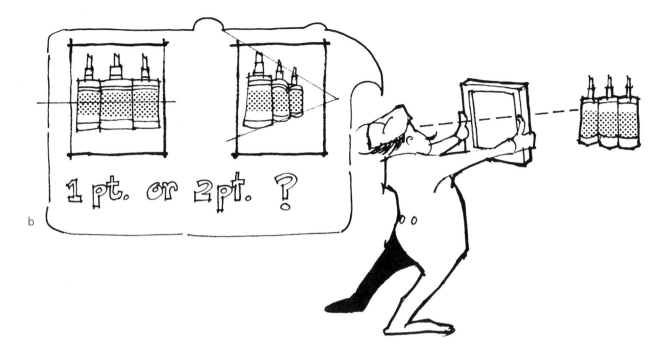

1 pt. or 2pt. ?

b

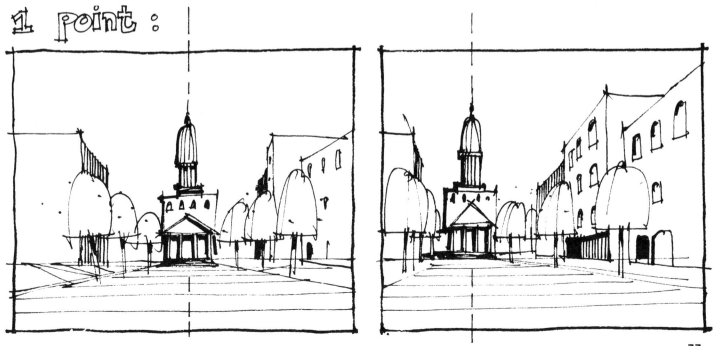

1 point :

a

Two-point Perspective

Two-point perspective goes beyond the frontal dimension, involving the side and back as well. It is the preferred method for expressing a complex subject. The fact that the sketch is nonfrontal creates a sharper tonal contrast between planes. It is an ideal setting for the generation of tension between subjects and thus stimulates eye movement and enlivens static statements. Avoid closeup views in two-point perspective, as they can be highly distorted and may result in a lack of continuity.

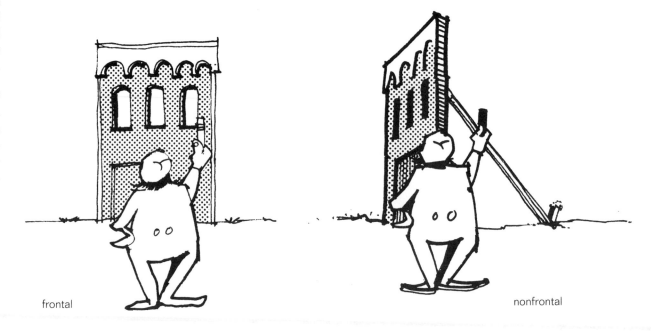

frontal

nonfrontal

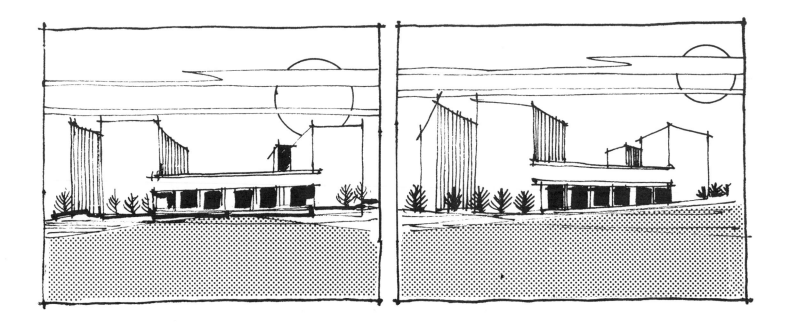

FRAMING

The four corners of the paper create dynamic interest and lead the eye away from the sheet. This situation should be corrected by reshaping the sheet with stoppers (Figure a), such as trees, bushes, rocks, human figures, or a corner of a building (Figure b). Their job is to form an edge perpendicular to the diagonal in order to prevent the eye from moving away from the point of interest. They also function as the foreground subject and should be rendered with bold and heavy strokes. Stoppers should always establish a strong tonal contrast with the rest of the picture. The position and type of stopper used should be studied carefully on thumbnail sketches (Figure c).

a   reasons for framing

b   types of framing

c   framing exercises

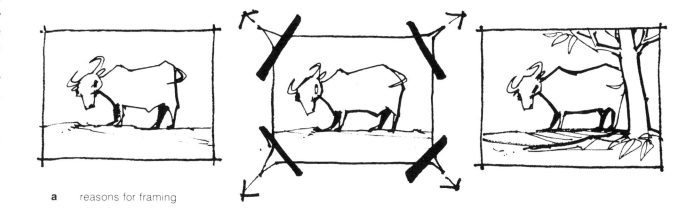

a   reasons for framing

b   types of framing

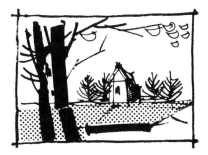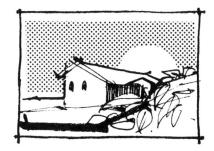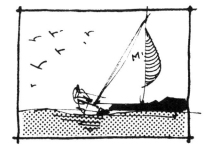

c   framing exercises

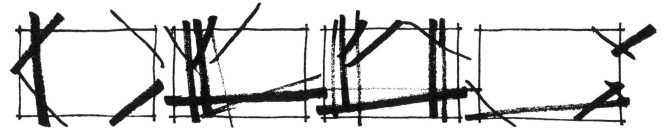

LIGHT EFFECTS

Light effects bring out the tonal contrast between planes and thus intensify the feeling of depth. They are also used to separate and classify the different layers of visual fields. For example, a house with a white roof will look sharper if it is placed in front of a dark background. Light effects are also used to define corners and spatial edges and to set a mood.

There are two kinds of realistic light sources, both with a definite direction. Natural light originates from one single source—the sun—and the light beams are parallel. Artificial light has a radiating pattern and can emanate from more than one source. In sketching, a *chiaroscuro* style can also be used. This is a pictorial representation of light, rather than a realistic interpretation of the source and its behavior. It is used to achieve a certain mood and atmosphere and yields an effective and abstract expression of light if done correctly.

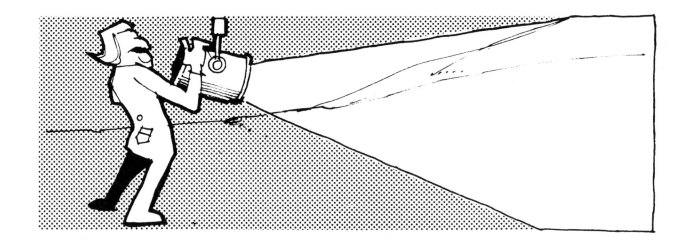

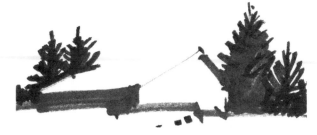

use of texture to differentiate the planes

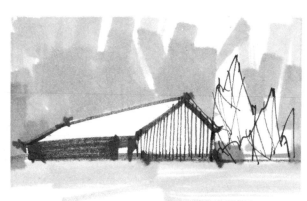

trees in background help define the shape of the roof

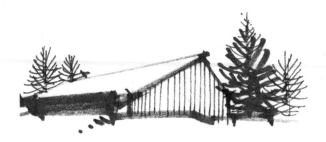

use of zip-a-tone as background tone

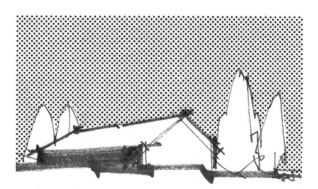

use of gray as background to bring out the contrast

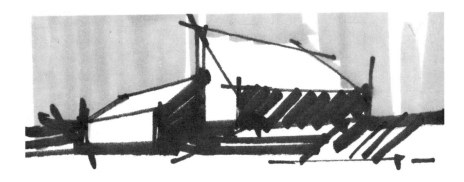

light source from left, gray background,
shaded side of building black, emphasis on
the building

foreground tree black, house and background
light, exaggerated distance in between

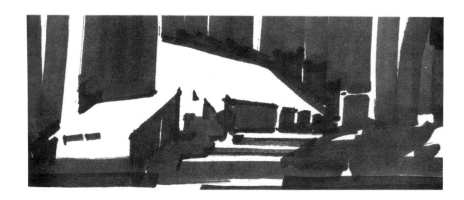

background black, roof white, strong
contrast, striking and strong mood

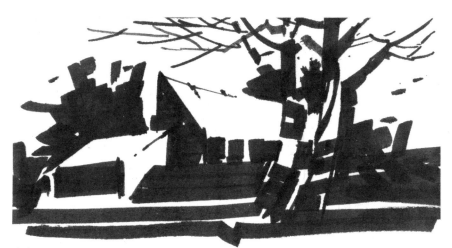

light source not consistent, emphasis on the
sculptural effect of the building creates
special effect

Light Intensity

Light intensity is graphically represented by different colors or different values of one color. Its quality varies on all surfaces and sometimes even on the same surface, depending upon the position and angle of the viewer. The spot with maximum reflection usually appears to be lighter and brighter. A long, continuous surface can exhibit a variety of intensities, due to interference from other objects and the texture of the surface from which the light is reflected. Three-dimensional forms should be obvious from the ways in which light and shadow fall upon them. Shadow should be used to direct eye movement. The path of light and shadow should be carried from border to border. Use strong basic shapes to define the shadow pattern. Don't attempt to capture a realistic pattern—this is the job of a camera. A sketch is not a photograph!

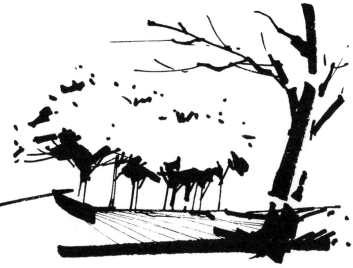

strong contrast of foliage suggests the roundness of the tree canopy

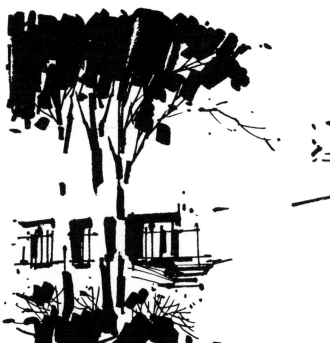

dark tree canopy and shrubs in the foreground create a perfect setting for viewers to look into

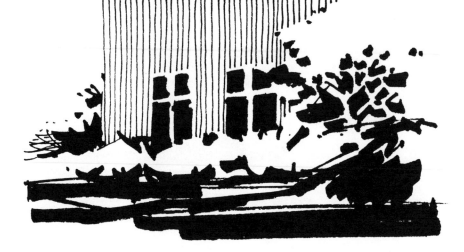

bold and dark horizontal lines in the foreground tend to lead the eye movement, creating contrasting patterns with the vertical texture on the wall

Expression of Light Effect

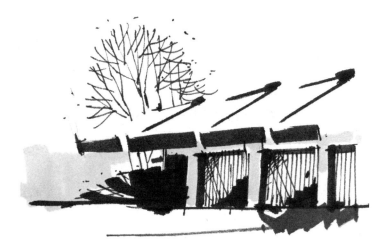

contrast in tone emphasizes the connection
between the house and the roof

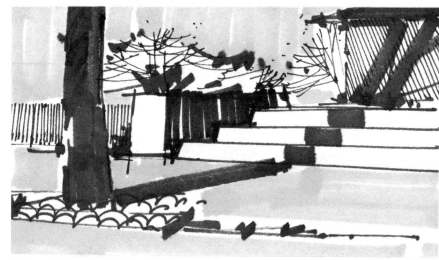

shadow of tree promotes diagonal eye movement across the page and leads viewers to
the theme (house)

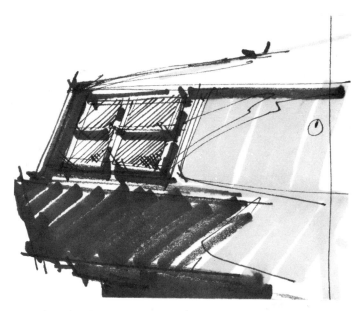

renders details and the reflection of light

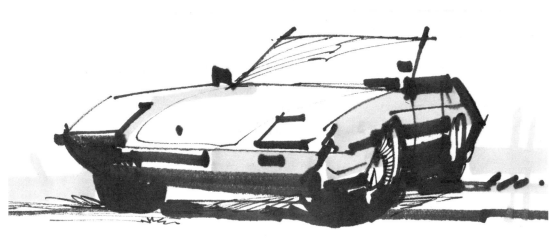

brings out the sculptural effect of the product

A SUCCESSFUL SKETCH

A good sketch is like a breath of fresh air. Looking at it should be an enlightening experience. The subject matter should be interesting, the composition should be appropriate and pleasing, and viewers must be able to see themselves in the picture rather than functioning merely as onlookers. The line should be forceful and should flow in a meaningful way. The strokes of the marker and the colors you use should evoke a sense of relaxation and freedom.

Sketch beyond the four borders of the sheet. Allow the lines to flow and extend beyond the page. The most unconstructive habit in sketching is to confine yourself within a fixed border. Marker movement should be fast and precise. Avoid hesitation, which can cause bleeding and uneven line width. Let the marker rotate freely at your fingertip. Acquire a good sense of scale, proportion, and perspective, and other skills will come automatically with practice.

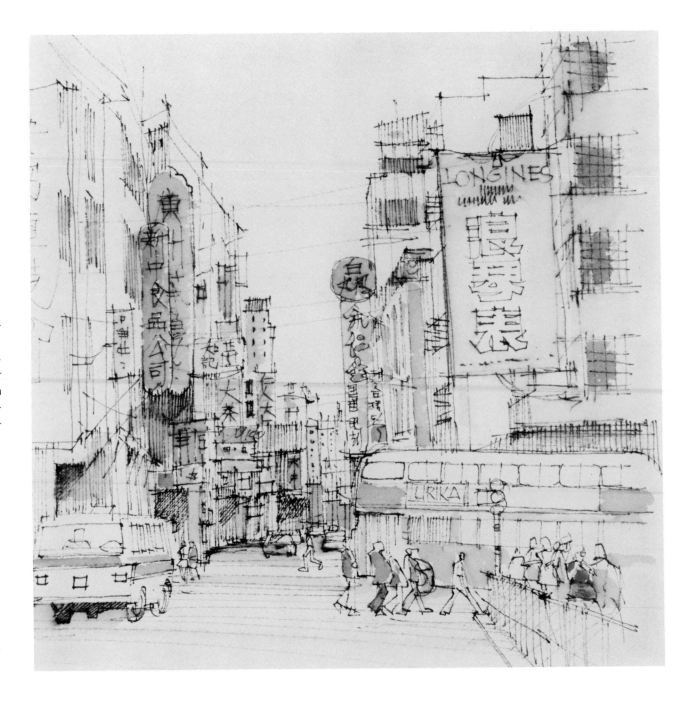

Title: Kowloon, Hong Kong
Original size: 8½ x 11 inches
Medium: Pilot fine-line and watercolor marker on watercolor paper
Technique: line drawing and wash

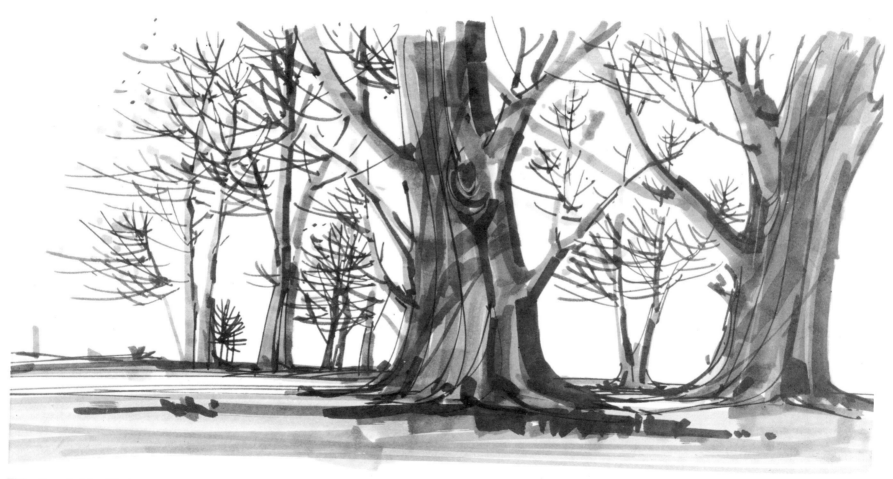

Title: Toronto Island Park
Original size: 8½ x 11 inches
Medium: color marker on bristol board
Technique: fine branches were outlined
with brown ultra-fine nib

DEMONSTRATION III

color marker on Aquabee felt-tip marker paper

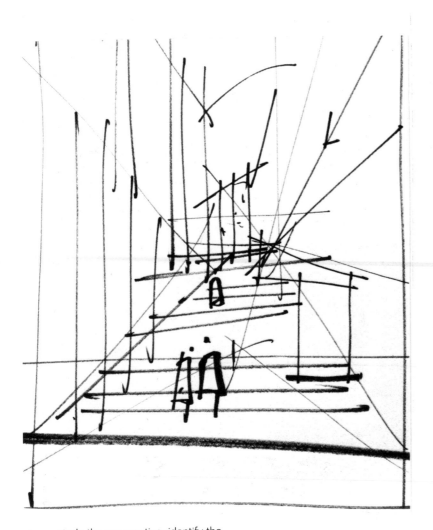

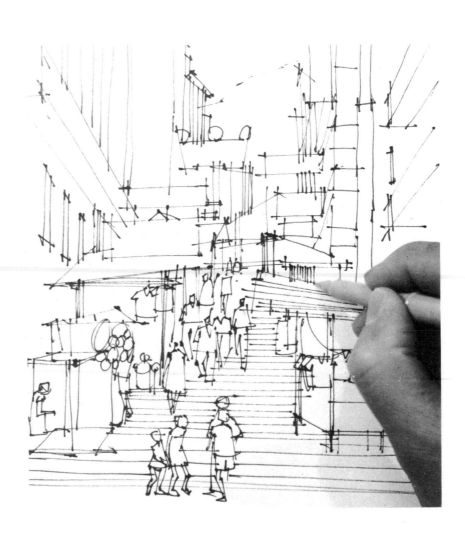

a   study the perspective; identify the
horizon and all the reference planes; pay
attention to the change in elevation and the
shift of vanishing point from the horizon to
the top of the steps; lay out with pencil and a
thin marker

b   sketch the general outline with a Pilot
razor-point marker; capture the major
elements first; no details

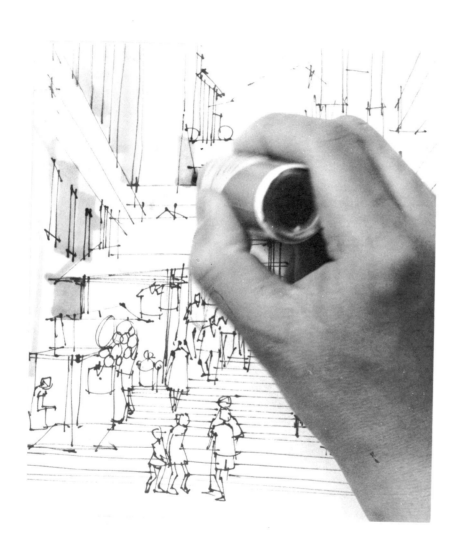

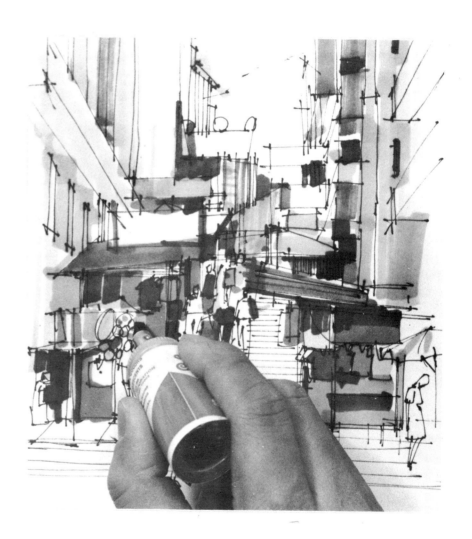

c   apply the first coat of color; use lighter colors for base, apply with broad strokes; move quickly over the paper; and don't worry about going over the predrawn edges

d   build up the three-dimensional quality by applying darker values and grays

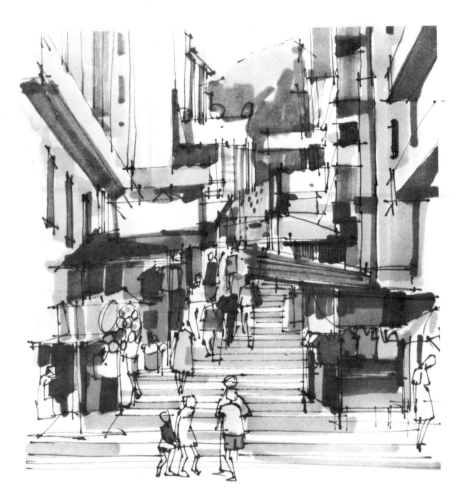

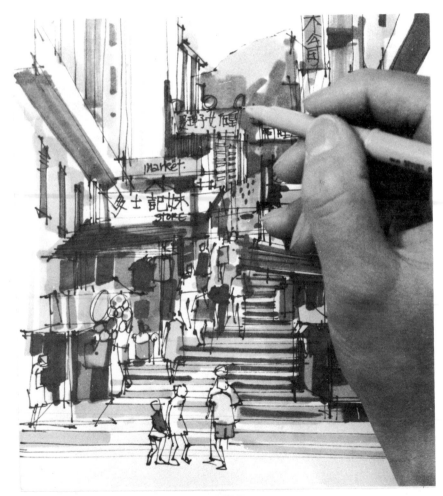

e   add accent colors to people, signs, and
decorative ornaments; add grays and black to
the shaded sides; add shadows

f   sharpen the spatial edges and details
with a fine-point marker; redefining edges
may be necessary due to marker bleeding

Title: Old Cairo, Egypt
Original size: 14 x 17 inches
Medium: Eberhard Faber markers on rice paper, watercolor
Technique: use black marker to outline the sketch; wash with black and gray; highlight the figure with bright color

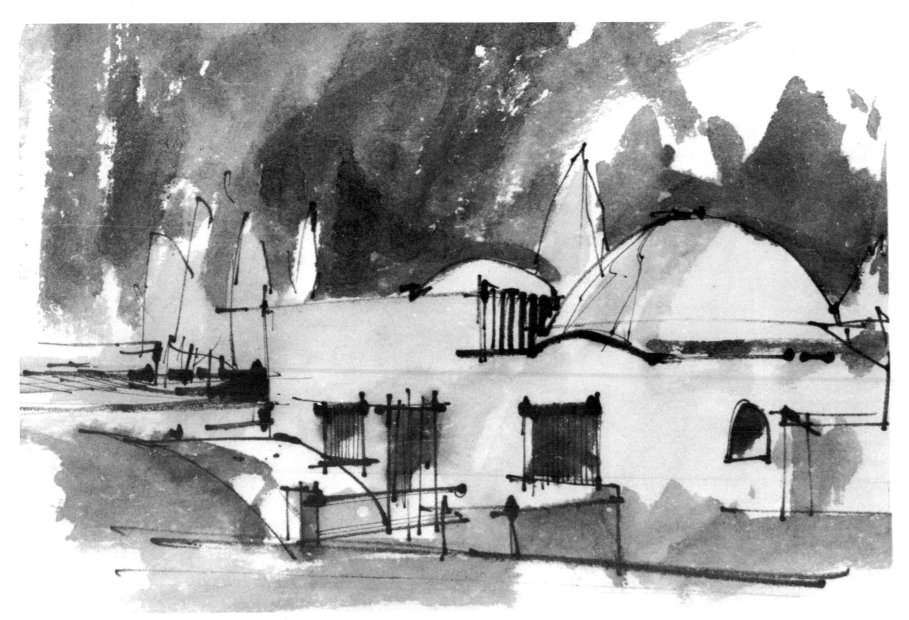

Title: Egyptian Farm House, Cairo
Original size: 11 x 17 inches
Medium: Eberhard Faber on rice paper,
blacks and olive green watercolor
Technique: sketch with markers; use broad
brush strokes to fill in the spaces; highlight
the trees with light olive green

DEMONSTRATION IV

Eberhard pointed-nib on rice paper

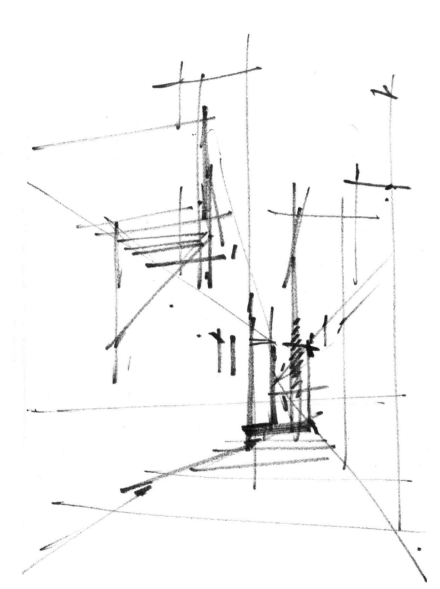

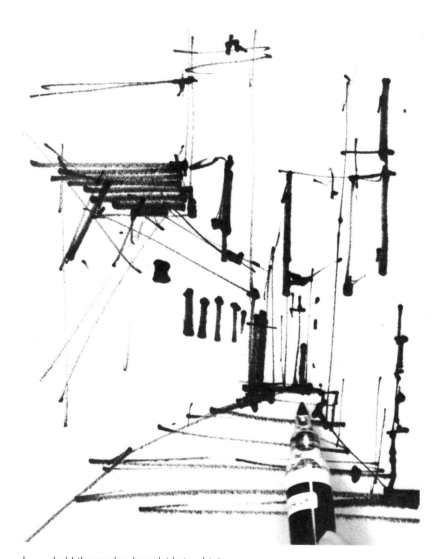

a   outline the scene with quick strokes;
know exactly the locations of reference
planes

b   hold the marker broadside to obtain
thicker line width; lift the marker off the paper
immediately after every stroke

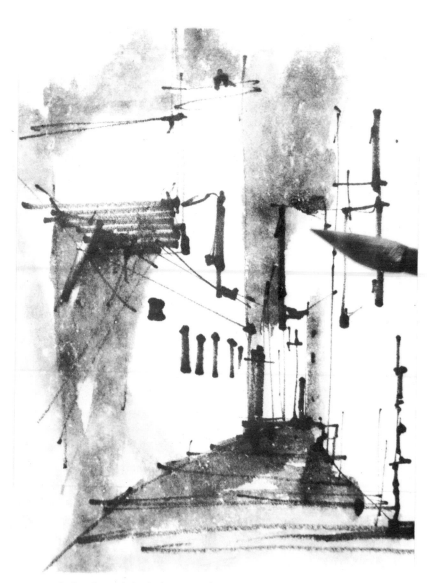

c   wash the sky and shaded areas with
light gray ink; leave planes facing the sun
white; let dry

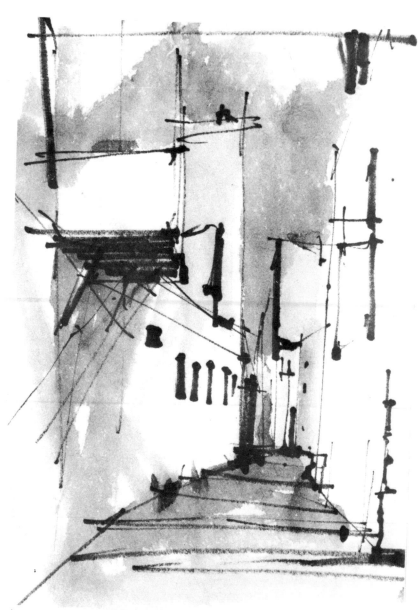

d   sharpen spatial edges with the pointed-
nib marker; then it's done; hands off; don't
overdo it

DEMONSTRATION V

fine-line marker, watercolor on watercolor paper

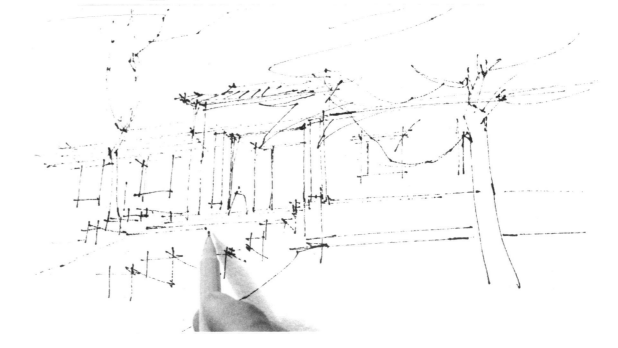

a   outline the scene with a Pilot razor-
point marker; avoid details

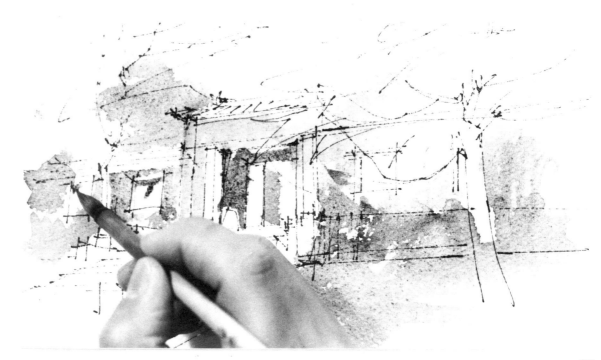

b   apply watercolor; lighter colors always
go first; gradually apply darker values after
preceding coat is dried; be patient

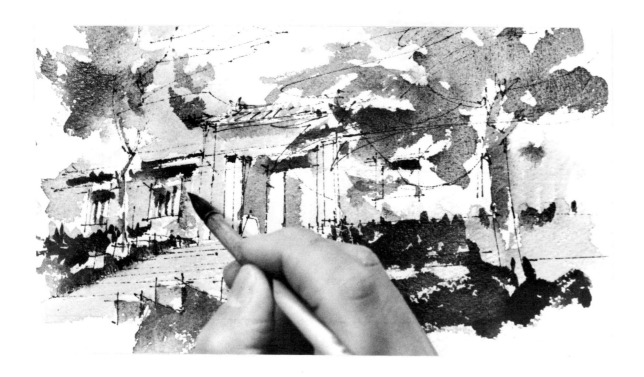

c   apply darker tones to bring out the shadows and depth

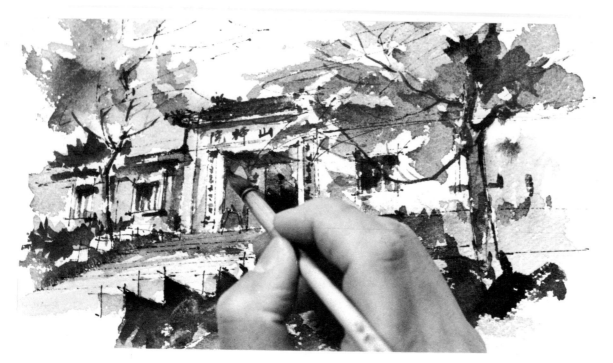

d   sharpen details with a fine-point marker; add accent color (marker) for highlighting

94

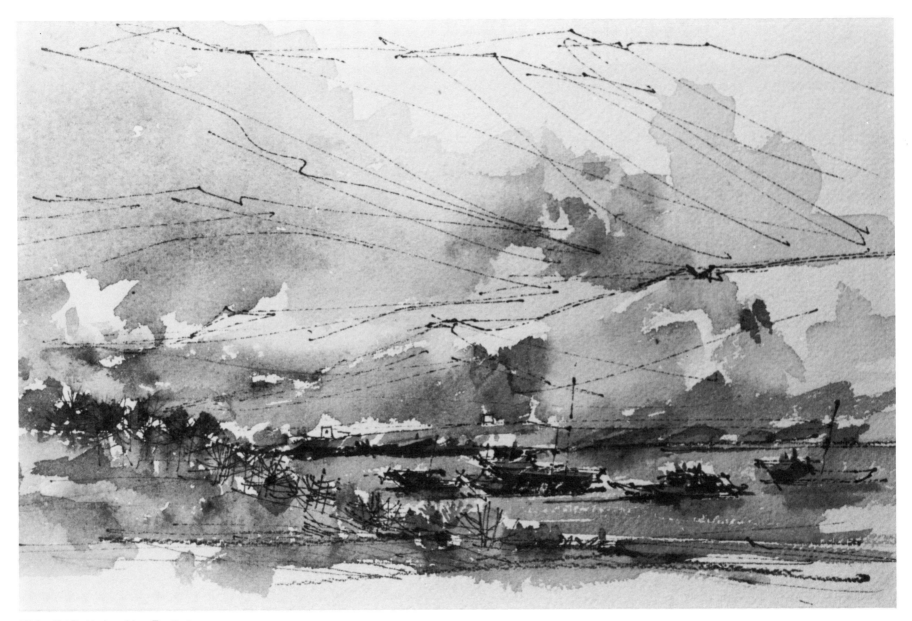

Title: Tai Po Harbor, New Territories,
Hong Kong
Original size: 11 x 9 inches
Medium: Pilot fine-line marker, watercolor
on watercolor paper
Technique: watercolor wash on line
drawing

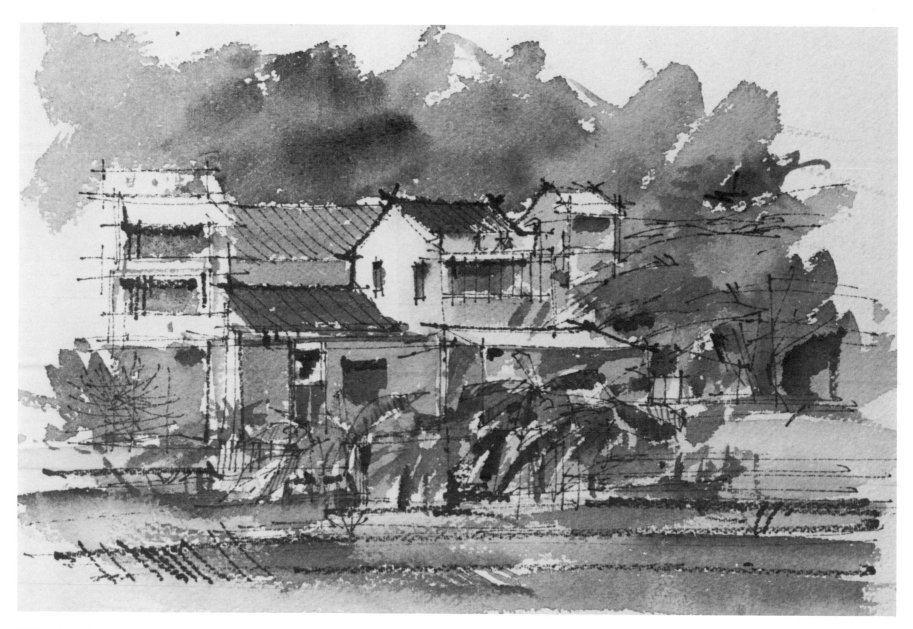

Title: studio demonstration
Original size: 11 x 17 inches
Medium: color marker on watercolor paper
Technique: Eberhard Faber pointed-nib
marker used to outline important spatial
edges

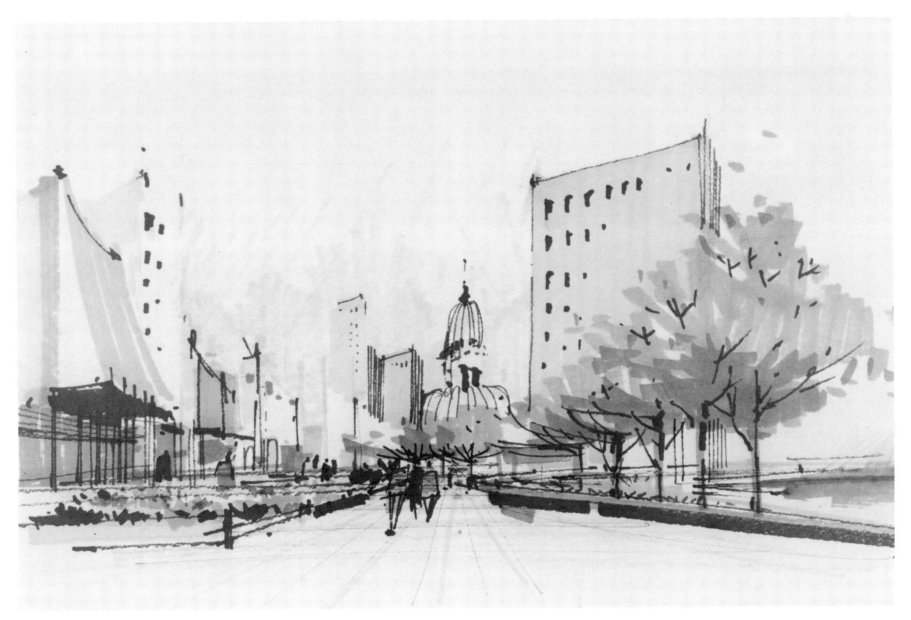

Title: Tai Po Village, New Territories,
Hong Kong
Original size: 9 x 11 inches
Medium: Pilot fine-line marker and
watercolor on watercolor paper
Technique: watercolor wash on line
drawing, heavy black line drawn with
Eberhard Faber pointed nib

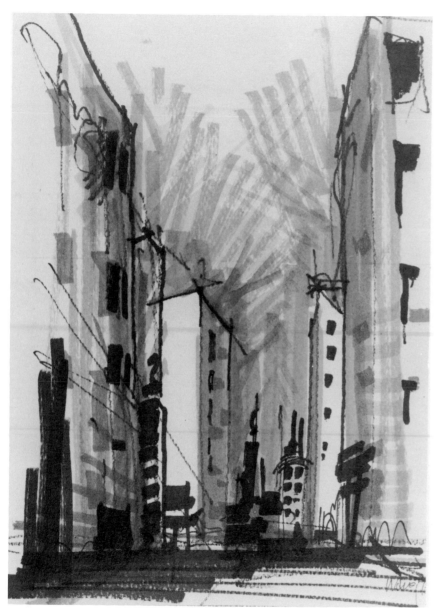

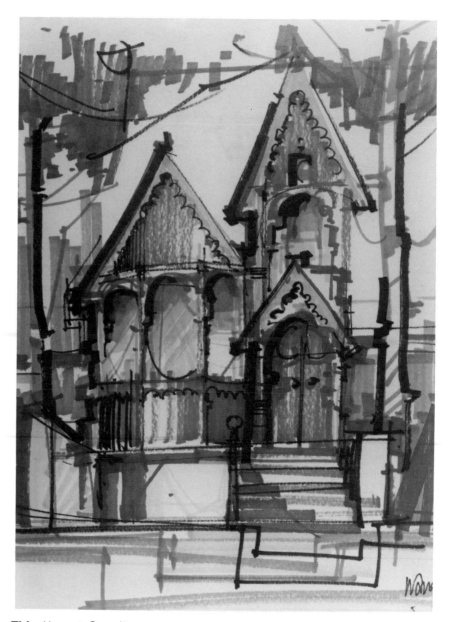

Title: Downtown
Original size: 11 x 9 inches
Medium: color marker on watercolor paper
Technique: broad marker strokes

Title: House in Sausalito
Original size: 11 x 14 inches
Medium: color marker on watercolor paper
Technique: broad marker strokes

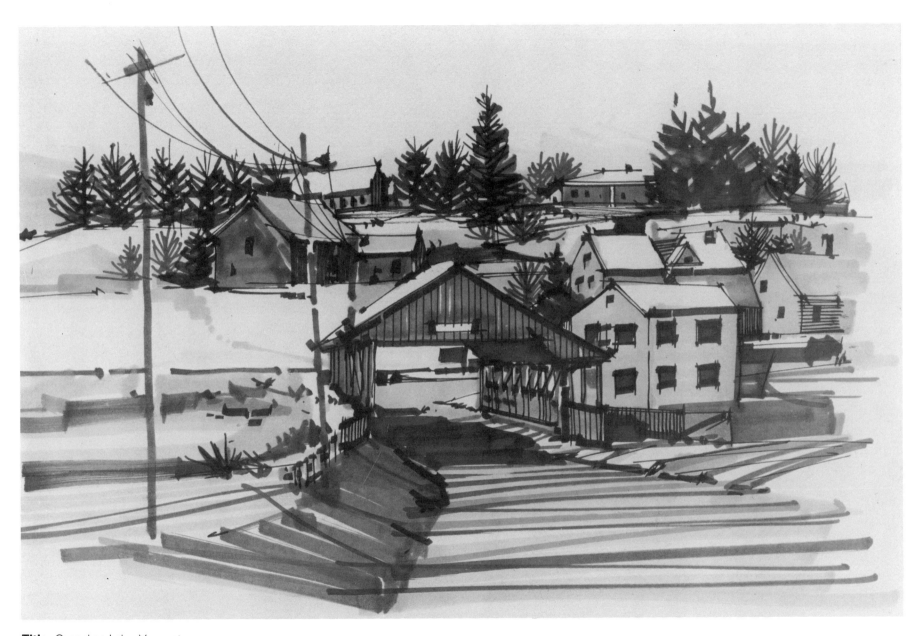

Title: Queechee Lake, Vermont
Original size: 9 x 11 inches
Medium: black and gray marker on
bristol board
Technique: broad strokes

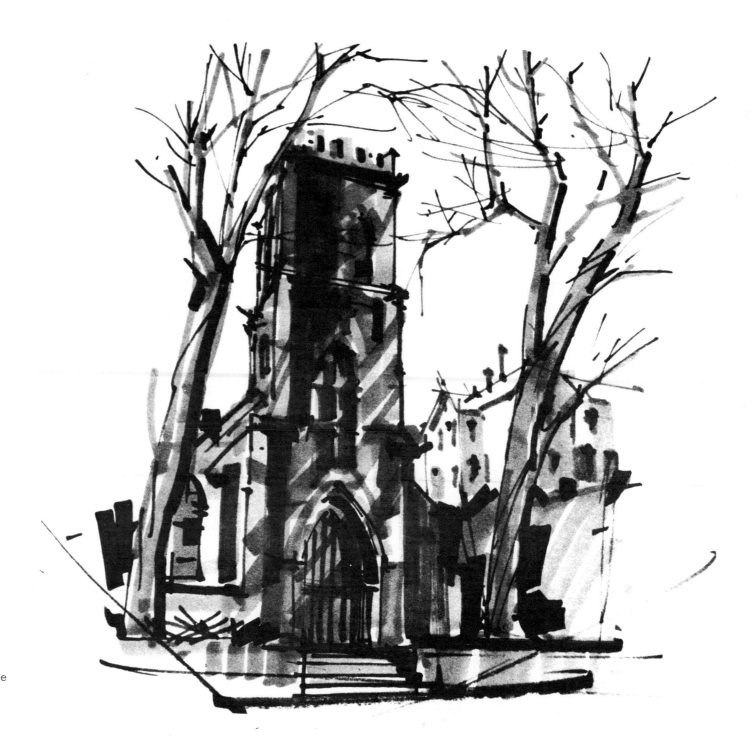

Title: Church in Galina, Illinois
Original size: 11 x 14 inches
Medium: color marker on Aquabee
felt-tip-marker paper
Technique: broad strokes

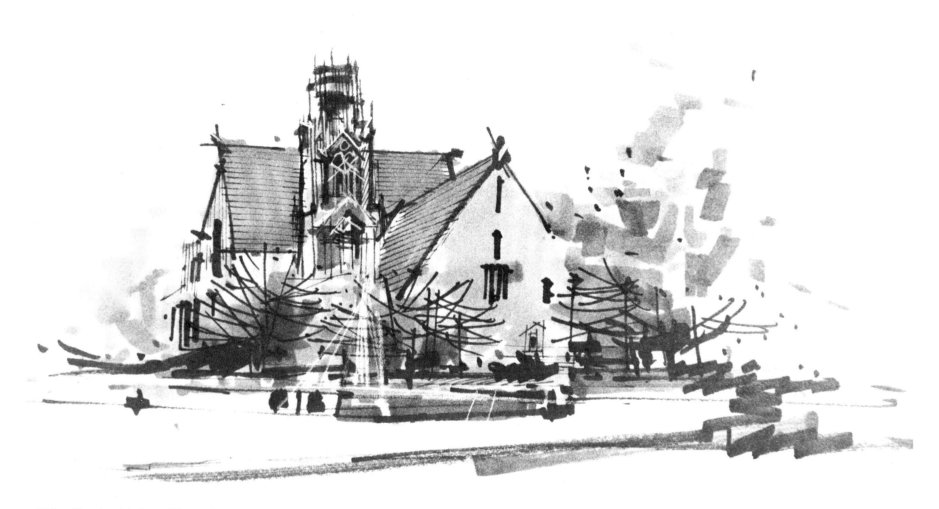

Title: Church in Madison, Wisconsin
Original size: 11 x 14 inches
Medium: color marker on Aquabee
felt-tip-marker paper
Technique: broad strokes

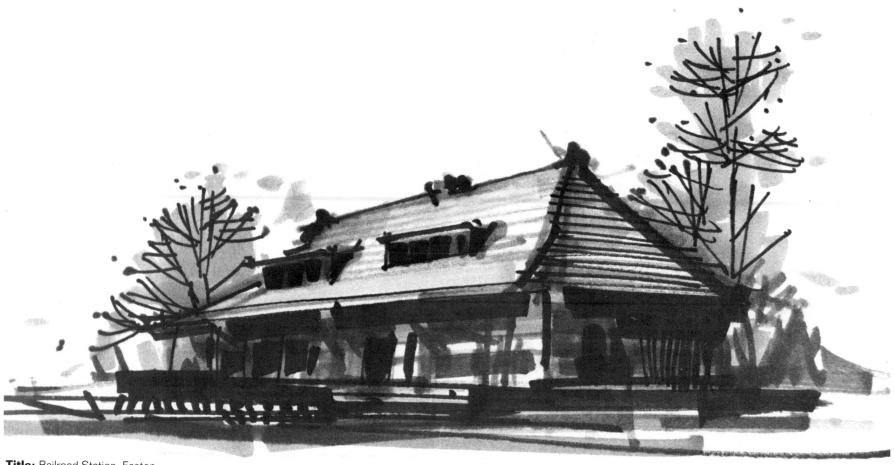

Title: Railroad Station, Easton,
Massachusetts
Original size: 11 x 14 inches
Medium: color marker on Aquabee
felt-tip-marker paper
Technique: broad strokes

INDEX